Bringing School to Life

Bringing School to Life

Place-Based Education Across the Curriculum

Sarah K. Anderson

ROWMAN & LITTLEFIELD
Lanham • Boulder • New York • London

Published by Rowman & Littlefield
A wholly owned subsidiary of The Rowman & Littlefield Publishing
Group, Inc.
4501 Forbes Boulevard, Suite 200, Lanham, Maryland 20706
www.rowman.com

Unit A, Whitacre Mews, 26-34 Stannary Street, London SE11 4AB

British Library Cataloguing in Publication Information Available

Library of Congress Cataloging-in-Publication Data

Names: Anderson, Sarah K., 1976- author.
Title: Bringing life to school : place-based education across the curriculum
  / Sarah K. Anderson.
Description: Lanham : Rowman & Littlefield, [2017] | Includes
  bibliographical references.
Identifiers: LCCN 2017032029 (print) | LCCN 2017036595 (ebook) | ISBN
  9781475830620 (electronic) | ISBN 9781475830606 (hardcover : alk. paper) |
  ISBN 9781475830613 (pbk. : alk. paper)
Subjects: LCSH: Place-based education. | Interdisciplinary approach in
  education.
Classification: LCC LC239 (ebook) | LCC LC239 .A55 2017 (print) | DDC
  370.115—dc23
LC record available at https://lccn.loc.gov/2017032029

Printed in the United States of America

For My Mother

Contents

Foreword

Sarah Anderson is the real deal. By which I mean, she knows what she's talking about. Place-based education is finally coming into its own after a decade or two of lurking around the edges of American educational pedagogy. Nowadays, school administrators from Brooklyn to Oakland, Maryland, to Atlanta to McCall, Idaho, to San Francisco to Portland have seen the virtues of this approach that invigorates students, teachers, and parents. This book documents that invigoration. In her preface, Sarah describes an activity in which "the air is electric with excitement and discovery as the students continue on their slug scavenger hunt." American classrooms need more electric excitement and slug scavenger hunts!

Sarah has earned her stripes as a middle school social studies teacher and now as the Fieldwork and Place-Based Education Coordinator for 10 years at the Cottonwood School of Civics and Science in Portland, Oregon. One of the guiding values at the school is to encourage *authentic, place-based learning*, by which they mean this:

> Children learn best when participating in authentic, hands-on learning experiences that are closely tied to the community. Our place-based approach improves student achievement, helps students develop a closer connection with the community in which they live, creates an appreciation for the natural world, and cultivates a desire to serve as active and committed citizens.

Sarah's portrait of this work crackles with the excitement of students unearthing the history of Oregon's civil rights policies, building models of Chinook longhouses to display at Portland State University's Archaeology Roadshow, advocating for a dog poop ordinance in front of the city council, designing a Mexican restaurant in the classroom, and on and on. This book is the maturation of an educational movement that has been growing over the past 20 years. Let me provide a bit of historical context.

One of the early initiatives in place-based education, the CO-SEED project, took root in rural northern New England schools in New Hampshire and Vermont. With my colleagues Delia Clark and Bo Hoppin at Antioch University New England, we worked with schools to ground their learning in their local places with a focus on the natural and cultural heritage of their communities. Our goal was to make school more relevant, more compelling, more engaging through planting gardens, interviewing seniors, reviving downtowns, studying the stream that coursed by the edge of the playground but was normally off-limits. We hoped to create an alternative school change model.

The dominant school change paradigm in the late 1990s and the first decade of the 21st century was, to quote Sarah Palin, "Drill, baby, drill." She was talking about oil policy, but the statement also applied to the focus in American schools on increasing academic achievement through memorization, endless worksheets and tedious drilling, and testing. Instead, we wanted to show that increased academic achievement would more effectively be accomplished through getting out of the classroom and into the real world on the school grounds, around the neighborhood, and in the community. Moreover, we wanted to demonstrate that solely focusing on academic achievement was a meager goal. We aspired to academic achievement in concert with citizen development, community vitality, and environmental improvement.

Regional foundations took notice of our work and said, "Well, we like what you're doing in rural schools with mostly white kids. But how about taking this downtown and working with diverse inner city schools?" And so we brought our school improvement approach to schools in and around Boston—in Malden, Jamaica Plain, Dorchester. At first, we thought it would be harder. But we quickly realized that the array of cultural resources, businesses, and knotty problems made a place-based approach in urban settings way more interesting.

In rural New England, where schools are often relocated away from village centers, the nearby neighborhood is mostly buggy marshes, chickadees, and sometimes a cemetery. Down the block from Boston schools were museums, the neighborhood bodega, shelters for homeless women offering urban gardening and aquaculture, historical sculptures. Yes, the playgrounds were paved and often ungreen, but city parks and undeveloped lots held interesting potential.

Sarah's book is the maturation of this movement to take place-based education downtown, into the heart of the city. A similar place-based initiative at a school in Providence, Rhode Island, led administrators to realize that the teachers, much less the students, didn't really understand the city's history and nature. As a result, they started to implement professional development focused on the idea of Learning Providence—visits to art and history museums, presentations by local nonprofits, cemetery tours, field trips to restaurants sourcing their menu items locally.

Similarly, Sarah's book is about Learning Portland—from both the teacher and student perspectives. In the early grades, children become experts in local plants: elderberry, snowberry, Oregon grape, black cottonwood, dogwood, licorice fern, sword fern, mock orange, piggyback plant, and salmonberry. In the middle school grades, students learn that the civil rights movement didn't just happen in the South, but that there's a long, uncomfortable history of segregation, restrictive legislation, and residential redlining right in their own backyards. Encounters with homeless people on local walking field trips lead to a curriculum on the causes of homelessness with presentations in the classrooms by current and past neighborhood victims of homelessness. Like peeling back the layers of an onion, teachers realize that an infinite set of possibilities exists right around the block.

This book is both provocative and practical. Provocative in that I suspect you'll often find yourself thinking, "Never would have thought of that as a curriculum project!" Hosting a naturalization ceremony at the school, students as technology tutors at a nearby senior living facility, and "teaching lunch" to overcome some of the uncomfortable social dynamics of the lunchroom were just a few of my *aha!* moments. Practical in that Sarah gets down to the nuts and bolts of what you've got to do to get started. I appreciated her list of things you'll need in your classroom to do place-based projects—a classroom set of clip-boards, a phone with a speaker option, easily rearrangeable furniture, digital cameras, and audio recorders. Useable advice.

Most of all, I appreciate her emphasis on developing citizens—students who will grow up to be active contributors in their communities. Dewey's concept of schools as "laboratories of democracy" is elegantly illustrated in Sarah's portrait of the Cottonwood School. Voting, activism, empathy for the needy, persuasive writing, techniques for environmental advocacy, public speaking, letters to the editor, and conflict resolution are all core skills that are cultivated there.

Jose Massé, one of the founders of the similar place-based Young Achievers Math and Science Pilot School in Boston, described the school's students, saying, "From an early age, they understand the idea of civic engagement—not to be bystanders, but to be active in changing things they believe need to be changed. That has to be part of the pedagogy in schooling if we're going to be successful in the 21st century." After nine years at the Cottonwood School, students graduate as engaged citizens of Portland, of Oregon, of the world. Take this wise book by Sarah Anderson into your heart and use it to make your school a better place.

—David Sobel, MEd
Teaching Faculty, Education
Antioch University
Author of *Place-Based Education:
Connecting Classrooms and Communities*

Preface

Spring in the Willamette River Valley. The southwest hillsides of Portland, Oregon, blush a pastel green as the urban canopy gently unfolds. Low, heavy clouds trundle in from the Pacific Ocean, sometimes dropping a misty rain, sometimes releasing a downpour. Once in a while, a much-anticipated burst of sunlight breaks through. Flowers are everywhere: popping up next to sidewalks, brightening trees, filling gardens and empty lots. Even in the heart of the city, spring pulses.

The South Waterfront is a new district in Portland. A few decades ago, this strip of land was bustling with shipbuilding yards, but after that, the area lay empty and abandoned. Now this stretch of city on the banks of the Willamette River is home to growing businesses and residential buildings, based at the foot of Portland's largest employer, Oregon Health and Science University. Over the past 10 years, several high-rise apartment buildings have gone up, and even more are being planned. At the very south end of this new neighborhood, tucked into an old industrial building that it shares with a heated storage business, is the Cottonwood School of Civics and Science.

On this spring afternoon, only half the students are in their classrooms working on projects. If you follow the streetcar line a few miles north to the Portland State University campus, you will find members of the 3rd grade class behind their booth at the Archaeology Roadshow. They are in the midst of displaying a 3-D model of a Chinook longhouse, which they built alongside a model of an archeological site. You can identify a site where a shelter once stood, they explain, by the fire circle burnt in the center. Students also direct visitors to a large map showing natural resources used by local tribes. A tub of water sits in front of the exhibit, next to a bucket of cedar planks. Students encourage visitors to experiment with the cedar in water to get an idea as to why it was such an essential building material for the Chinook.

Heading directly south from the university and winding along the tree-covered length of Terwilliger Boulevard, you will find another group of students busily engaged at Tryon Creek State Park. The 6th grade class has made many forays into this forest over the school year—to explore, to learn, and to help. One highlight has been the "ivy pulls"—when the class works together to remove the invasive and smothering English ivy from trees and the forest floor. Another highlight has been their visits to research banana slugs, one of the forest's primary decomposers.

Today, the 6th graders are here to teach their 1st and 2nd grade buddies what they have learned about banana slugs. The teams work together to find and map slugs along their route. The older students huddle on the ground with their young mentees, pointing out features on the decomposers and helping to identify their location on the map. The air is electric with excitement and discovery as the students continue on their slug scavenger hunt.

Going north again, we shift our attention to the heart of downtown: city hall. In the council chambers, 7th and 8th graders sit in the wings, getting ready to give testimony. For the past several months, this group has investigated the topic of secondhand smoke in public parks: the scientific research, policy examples from other cities, and statistical results from their own surveys. Today, the city council is hearing public comments on the issue for a vote the following week. The students are called to the mic. They walk forward, nervous, but confident. They are ready.

The snapshots above illustrate not only a place, but a holistic approach to raising informed, compassionate children who care about the communities where they live. These are real examples primarily from my experience as a place-based educator in a small charter school in Portland.

I did not grow up in Oregon. I spent my childhood and much of my young adulthood in northern Vermont, where people seem to be born with a fierce sense of place. I completed my student teaching across the

Connecticut River, in a small and struggling old factory town in New Hampshire.

After observing the middle school classes there for a few days, I concluded that this was a community in crisis. The classes did not engage students, and the kids often treated their teachers with disrespect. The teachers clearly felt overwhelmed and frustrated. There seemed to be very little learning going on. The kids were bored and couldn't see any reason for school, so they naturally became disconnected and, I would argue, disenfranchised. The school did not actively work to connect the students to the town or the real issues taking place locally.

This seemed like a true disservice, both to the students and to the town. These kids were, after all, the future citizens and stewards of this place. How could they prepare to take over this essential role if they did not have a chance to practice it, if they were never taught how to care for their place, if they did not have the opportunity to love it?

Place has become central to my teaching practice. There is nothing more concrete—more *real*—than the piece of earth and the communities where we live. Place both grounds us and connects us. When we give our children the opportunity to know their environments through exploration, investigation, play, work, service, and restoration, we allow them to fully experience life firsthand, and in the process learn more than they ever could in a classroom.

WHY THIS BOOK?

David Sobel eloquently describes this refreshing and innovative way of teaching in his book, *Place-Based Education: Connecting Classrooms and Communities*. It is the perfect primer on the topic, filled with research and examples. Not only does Sobel outline the underlying philosophy, he also offers strategies for initiating programs, addressing academic achievement, and building strong partnerships. Greg Smith and Sobel followed up with *Place- and Community-Based Education in School*, which gives even more details, examples, and background research. Both authors have spent a majority of their careers developing and researching place-based education in schools and communities.

This book is not meant as a primary text on place-based education but as an extension. Much of the content comes from my experience as a middle school teacher who has implemented place-based education for 10 years, as well as examples from other teachers at my school. The intention is to give other educators tips and ideas on how to craft place-based education curriculum and build a place-based school, using the Cottonwood School of Civics and Science as an illustrative example. Hopefully, this book will paint a clear picture of what place-based education looks like, so that it can more easily translate from a good *idea* to a successful *practice*.

WHY A CHARTER SCHOOL?

In 2006, Portland Public Schools closed Smith Elementary School in Southwest Portland. A group of parents decided to apply for a charter with the hope of keeping a public elementary school in their neighborhood. In the process of researching, proposing, and fighting for their vision, the group discovered a love for civic engagement. They decided to transfer this newfound passion to the guiding philosophy for the charter and learned that place-based education perfectly fit with what they wanted to do. Since then, we have been carefully developing our program and coming to a better understanding of what it means to be a place-based school.

There are other schools in Oregon and around the country that have a place-based mission, and many of them are charter schools. One reason is because charters are often smaller than traditional public schools and have more autonomy over decisions like curriculum. Like us, some of these schools also pursued charters as a way to keep their doors open in response to the threat of closure, often from underenrollment in rural areas.

There has been much debate over charter schools since their origin and even more so recently due to our current political climate. Many feel that the lottery systems used by charters make them exclusive and unattainable for most. Others feel that charters drain public school districts of valuable dollars and resources.

One of the earliest advocates for charters, Albert Shanker, envisioned them as independently managed schools focused on educational experimentation and innovation. Within this democratic model, teachers have more of a voice in how the school is run and the student body is more economically and racially integrated than other public schools.[1]

Much of the vision Shanker outlined in the 1980s and 1990s has not been fully realized. He was a big advocate of unions, and most charter schools are not unionized. He wanted charter schools to serve the most at-risk students in a community, which is not always the case—many charters serve middle-class kids with solid neighborhood school alternatives. And when Shanker saw that states allowed charters to be used as for-profit venues, he turned against them.[2]

Oregon requires that its charter schools be not-for-profit. The language of the original state law is in line with Shanker's ideas. The Oregon legislature intended charter schools to "be created as a legitimate avenue for parents, educators and community members to take responsible risks to create new, innovative and more flexible ways of educating children within the public school system."[3]

Charters are granted to schools that propose curricula distinctly different from the typical neighborhood schools. Once a charter has established itself successfully, it is charged with disseminating what it has learned: "It is the intent that public charter schools may serve as models and catalysts for the improvement of other public schools and the public school system."[4] In this way, charters exist for the benefit and enrichment of the public at large. One of the responsibilities is to experiment and report back. Much of this book comprises such a report.

For the last few years, I have had the position of fieldwork and place-based education coordinator at the Cottonwood School. In this position, I coordinate fieldwork logistics for teachers, help them design place-based units, lead professional development trainings, and work to develop community partnerships. My focus is our mission as a place-based school.

In several instances in this book, I share examples of projects from the classrooms at the Cottonwood School. I have done my best to acknowledge the teachers who developed and led these units of study. When I use the pronoun *we*, it is because the teacher and I worked together to build the place-based component, or it is referring to a project I designed when I was the middle school humanities teacher.

A NOTE ABOUT THE WORD *CITIZEN*

When I use *citizen*, it is meant to identify a member of a community, town, or city. For example, we sometimes refer to students in our middle school classes as *citizens* of the class or of the school. In another context, the term *citizen scientist* is meant to denote a community member who is not a professional scientist but a person who is collecting data to contribute to ongoing research.

The reason I make this note is because some organizations and agencies that work with volunteers have revised their label of *citizen scientist* to *community scientist*. They have found that the word *citizen* can feel exclusive and even intimidating within some of the communities where they work. They want to make sure their language welcomes all residents who are interested in improving their neighborhoods and environment.

My use of the word *citizen* is certainly not meant to be exclusive in any way. I do not mean naturalized citizen or documented citizen of the United States. When I do want to make that distinction, I will specify by stating *American citizen*.

I didn't plan to be a teacher. After graduating from Bard College with a degree in American studies, I felt passionate about promoting democracy and increasing public involvement in decision-making. Helping people maintain a strong voice in planning and forming their own communities, as opposed to leaving the decisions to corporations and others who have no real investment in a place, especially interested me. After working with several nonprofit and government agencies, I inevitably realized that all real change comes through education. And as it turned out, I loved being a teacher.

Building a place-based school has been an exercise in experimentation. There are no step-by-step manuals or curricula packs to purchase. It can be messy and difficult, but it can also be tremendously fulfilling. This book is a guide via personal experience, even though my own work is still in process.

Schools are expected to do so much these days: teach a huge host of standards, prepare kids for careers, keep up with new technologies, and teach social skills. Raising informed citizens who will be ready for the job of maintaining democracy is yet another responsibility of public educators. But the good news is that teachers do not need to take all of this on alone. Like the saying goes, it takes a village. Place-based education literally turns to the community as a rich resource for teaching our young people while also allowing our children to become a valuable resource in their own right.

I have found that many people are routinely surprised by what kids can accomplish. My hope is that this book helps teachers make more connections and helps to give students an increased voice within their communities so that we can continue to astonish.

NOTES

1. Kahlenberg, Richard D., and Halley Potter. 2014. "The Original Charter School Vision." *New York Times*, August 30. Accessed May 5, 2017. https://www.nytimes.com/2014/08/31/opinion/sunday/albert-shanker-the-original-charter-school-visionary.html.

2. Ravitch, Diane. 2012. "How to Fix the Charter School Movement." *Washington Post*, July 16. Accessed May 5, 2017. https://www.washingtonpost.com/blogs/answer-sheet/post/how-to-fix-the-charter-school-movement-and-what-albert-shanker-really-said/2012/07/16/gJQAjxW4oW_blog.html.

3. Oregon Revised Statues 338.015. Accessed May 5, 2017. https://www.oregonlaws.org/ors/338.015.

4. Ibid.

Acknowledgments

This book is the product of many years of experience, first as a student and then as an educator. I have learned from so many talented teachers from high school to graduate school whose passion for community-minded education, grounded in social justice, inspired my own studies. I especially want to acknowledge Linda Rhodes, Mark Lytle, Sarah Willie, Jane Miller, and Murray McClellan. I am grateful to David Sobel, whose insightful writings and generous mentorship have guided my understanding of place-based education.

Throughout my development as an educator, several organizations have permitted me to create and conduct my own curriculum, allowing me to experiment with environmental education and place-based learning. Warm thanks to Hazen's Notch Association, the Salmon-Lermnitov family, Camp Caritas, and Smokey House Center.

My deep gratitude goes to the teachers at the Cottonwood School, some for reading, some for writing, and all for being innovative educators: Anne Gurnee, Amanda McAdoo, Emily Conner, Chris Wyland, Lisa Colombo, Morgen Kelm, Elizabeth Thompson, Susan Hathaway, Nesa Levy, Angie O'Brien, Raina Janke, Karinsa Kell, Paul Banta, and Courtney Miller. Much of their work is featured in this book.

A picture tells a story all its own. I extend appreciation to all students who granted permission to share their work in this book and all parent and teacher photographers who have allowed me to include their photos.

Thank you to Sarah Jubar for the supportive feedback and for helping me to navigate my first experience in book publishing.

Tremendous gratitude goes to Greg Smith for the insightful and honest feedback. His wisdom and guidance helped me piece ideas into an organized narrative and he consistently reminded me to focus on what is most important.

Thank you to Lucy Feit and Gilly Foley for providing additional and much-needed childcare. As always, I am indebted to my husband, David Schonfeld, for his editorial skills and willingness to support my writing schedule. My heartfelt gratitude to both him and our son for their encouragement and love.

CHAPTER 1

What Is Place-Based Education and Why Do We Need It Now?

One of the main goals of place-based education is to help raise citizens who understand how everyone and everything in a community is interconnected. Place-based education extends learning into both nature and the human-made aspects of a community. Learning revolves around environment, culture, economics, and governance.

Civic engagement is central to this approach. By working to make a difference in the places where they live, students develop civic knowledge, skills, and values while gaining even more motivation to make a difference.[1] This process imparts a sense of responsibility and encourages young people to be stewards of natural and cultural resources. It may also inspire them to propose and enact solutions to public problems.[2] Students can work both as individuals and as a part of collective efforts to bring positive change to the public sphere while deepening their understanding of the democratic process and how they are connected to the people and places around them.

In addition to civic engagement, students work to meet the needs that exist in their community through service learning (figure 1.1). These projects are not designed solely by the teacher but in collaboration with partner organizations and agencies. Service has many faces; students may research local history, collect data on neighborhood trees, plant snowberries, paint murals, or influence city policy. In all of these examples, though, young people become active, giving members of the community.

The place-based model overlaps and even incorporates several other educational approaches. It is helpful to define them briefly to see more

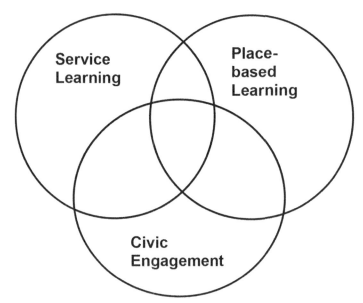

Figure 1.1.   The relationship of place-based education, civic engagement, and service learning.
Clark, Delia. 2008. Learning to Make Choices for the Future: Connecting Public
 Lands, Schools, and Communities through Place-based Learning and Civic En-
 gagement. Woodstock: VT: National Park Service Conservation Study Institute.
 Used with permission.

clearly where they intersect and how they are different. (The following is adapted from *Learning to Make Choices for the Future: Connecting Public Lands, Schools, and Communities through Place-Based Learning and Civic Engagement*" by Delia Clark.[3])

- Environmental Education: This can be any form of curricular materials or programs aimed at teaching students about the natural environment and how humans can take a more responsible, informed role in how we interact and care for the earth. As mentioned above, place-based education takes this platform and extends it to all aspects of a place, including the cultural, social, and economic.
- Project-Based Learning/Problem-Based Learning: Through project-based learning, students delve deep into a topic or a problem, often identified by the students. These projects can involve fieldwork, group/team work, and extensive research and problem-solving. Proj-

ects usually culminate in a product or presentation made by students for the class or school community. Place-based education's approach closely overlaps with project-based learning. A couple of differences are that place-based projects are rooted in the community and local issues (which is not necessarily the case for project-based), and place-based projects aim to incorporate civic education and service.

- Experiential Learning: Through this approach, students engage in direct experiences as opposed to just reading or hearing about other people's experiences. When students reflect on these experiences, new skills and attitudes develop. Place-based education is a kind of experiential learning, using the community as the basis for experience.
- Community-Based Learning: Using this method, students employ experiential learning, lifelong learning, service learning, and other strategies to access learning opportunities throughout their school, neighborhood, and wider community. Place-based education strives to establish a similar context for learning with the goal of developing civic responsibility and stewardship.
- Youth Voice: Many approaches to education, including project-based learning and service learning, value youth input as an essential component of harnessing interest and establishing student ownership. This could mean students help to choose, implement, and/or evaluate a project. Through this process, young people can find their voice and recognize that they have the power and the right to participate in even larger projects and decisions. Including youth voice in public decision making is a priority for place-based education.

These approaches overlap and support one another. Developing knowledge and skills via any of these methods will only strengthen a teacher's ability to successfully design and lead projects. The project is place based if it is strongly rooted in place (often multiple aspects of a place) with the aim of deepening students' civic knowledge through service to their community.

American philosopher and educator John Dewey planted the seeds for place-based learning more than 120 years ago when he wrote, "Education is a process of living, and not a preparation for future living."[4] Dewey reacted to schools that were set up as factories, churning out compliant workers. He knew that in a democracy it is crucial for public schools to prepare people to be citizens so that they can serve their communities, care for their land, and run their governments.

The urgency for experiential, hands-on "life learning" is just as imperative now as it was at the beginning of the 20th century. We need to continue taking down the walls between schools and the rest of the world. This requires a shift in our collective thinking. Schools are not just training grounds for children to learn content and job skills for 12 or more years before they are allowed back into broader society, ready to pursue their own individual enrichment. In the place-based education vision, schools and students become an integral *part* of the community acting for the public good.

For further reading about the history of place-based education and its defining components, see the Resources section at the end of this chapter.

WHY NOW IS THE TIME

There are multiple reasons why *now* is the right time for place-based education. Across the country, the stage is set for a new community-based, student-powered form of education.

Disconnection from Nature

Children are separated from the natural world more now than ever before. This crisis is well documented in *Last Child in the Woods*, wherein author Richard Louv labels the problem "nature-deficit disorder."[5] Kids are getting outside less and less often, partly because of the seductions of technology but almost more so because of parents who fear danger. The obvious result is a new generation that is less informed about the environment and, therefore, potentially less likely to care about it in the future. This inadvertently places more responsibility on schools to get students outside and into the natural world around them.

Revitalizing of Democracy

While it is essential that students learn about worldwide issues and understand the idea of global citizenship, it is also vital for them to know about what is right in front of them. Technology has made it easy for us to connect with people and places thousands of miles away and spend hours of our day immersed in alternate or virtual realities. The less time we spend learning about our own towns and cities, the less knowledge we have. This leads to us feeling less qualified to participate in the local democratic process. Civic engagement connects neighbors and puts students in touch with local issues.

It is as important for students to learn how their city government works as it is for them to know about the U.S. Constitution. Local politics often affect us more directly than national issues, even if the topics may not be as sensational. Additionally, students—and their parents—can get involved and make real change on a local level. Maintaining a democracy means giving young people the tools, information, and confidence they need to truly participate.

Need for a New Civic Education

The Annenberg Public Policy Center recently released the results of a poll that found that only 36 percent of Americans can name all three branches of government.[6] If American citizens don't understand how the government works, how can they actively participate or accurately reform? We are charged with a substantial responsibility to teach students the basics of how our government operates and our democracy functions.

Another study, this one from Northwestern University and Princeton University, found that the United States is no longer a democracy but is now an oligarchy.[7] Under this system of government, decisions and policies are not made by average citizens or for their benefit. The power is shifting. If citizens don't use their voices, they risk losing them altogether.

It is our responsibility as educators to balance the scales and ensure that our children will have a say in the future. It will be the children's responsibility to play a more active role in securing that future.

Cultivating Character

Social education has increasingly become a priority in classrooms and schools. As educators, we know that our charge is not just teaching the common core but showing kids how to be kind and compassionate, honest and respectful. When examining the purpose of place-based education, retired Lewis and Clark College education professor Greg Smith wonders what attributes people will need in order to "contribute to the resilience and adaptability of their communities in the face of climate change, resource exhaustion, and the social disintegration likely to become widespread in coming decades."[8]

Students working to improve their community naturally strengthens character. By actively engaging with their community, students learn to take responsibility for themselves and others. By gaining insight into diverse perspectives and experiences, students develop empathy. By performing collective acts of service, students learn to collaborate.

Long-term projects require perseverance and effective teamwork. They also demand patience and kindness. Presenting to authentic audiences comprised of invested adults builds both integrity and courage. Place-based education fosters the growth of caring and involved humans who recognize and value the ways in which we are all connected and depend on one another.

An Eye on Justice

One of our roles as educators in a democracy is to give students the tools they need to advocate for a better future. Our citizens need to be well-versed in American history, which includes the close study of times when we as a nation strayed from our mission of "liberty and justice for all."

Learning from our mistakes allows us to avoid similar injustices in the future and also gives students a context for current events and conflicts. By studying slavery in depth, students can see the roots of racial tensions today; by examining colonialism, we have a more informed understanding of recent conflict and global trade.

Likewise, looking at examples of compassionate leadership and courageous action gives young people models for own lives. For instance, it is important to know that most of the leaders in the civil rights movement were average, working-class citizens who felt compelled to stand against injustice. The more students can connect to such individuals from the past and recognize our common humanity, the more opportunities there are for young people to imagine themselves as agents of positive change.

Schools and Communities as Mutual Resources

Many of our communities are in crisis. Paul Nachtigal, former director of the Annenberg Rural Challenge, declared that "When school only focuses on how to benefit the individual, they become the enemy of the community. They educate young people to leave and so fulfill the prophecy that these places are doomed to poverty, decline and despair. Instead, we intend to rally communities to reinvent their schools as engines of renewal for the public good."[9]

As many rural areas across America lose industry, resources, and their young people, place-based education can offer a strategy for revitalization and renewal. By integrating school into the local towns, students work with partners to create or strengthen community programs and initiatives. Students develop a stronger bond with their place, rooted in experience and deep knowledge. The school and the students can even inspire local citizens to take a more active role. Place-based education recognizes that there is a link between healthy communities and a vital economy; when people are actively engaged, it attracts more people, and the hope is that the economy will follow.[10]

Although many examples of place-based education can be found in rural areas, the model can also fill a special niche in cities. As the American population becomes increasingly urban, more kids are going to school in densely populated areas. Inner-city areas may have just as much need for grassroots revitalization and community-building. Likewise, the city has a lot to offer to schools. Students can make better use of their local resources such as the public library, city hall, historical societies, public universities, and art museums. The city can literally become the classroom.

Making School Relevant

Student engagement is a concern for schools everywhere. Many educators are trying new strategies to combat high dropout rates. As David Perkins noted in his March 2016 *Educational Leadership* article

"Lifeworthy Learning," one way to keep students engaged now and for years to come is to make education more "lifeworthy."[11] In other words, student learning should not focus on isolated, abstract subjects but on larger, integrated topics that have relevant connections to students' lives, such as current events or local problems.

When engaged in a successful place-based education unit, students don't ask the age-old question, "Why do we need to learn this?" because the answer is obvious. Many times students don't even notice that they are learning because the education is so deftly camouflaged as real life.

Making learning more relevant has an impact beyond higher graduation rates. It provides a new role for schools within their community, one in which teachers and students actively contribute to civic improvement. Collaborating with colleagues and partner groups can be incredibly reinvigorating for teachers as well, and can help combat the feelings of isolation often reported by educators in traditional schools.[12]

Being the Mirror

The demographics of our nation are changing. The US Census Bureau predicts that by the year 2020, "more than half of the nation's children are expected to be part of a minority race or ethnic group."[13] Despite this trend in student populations, 82 percent of teachers are white. This is what the Center for American Progress and the National Education Association are calling a "diversity gap."[14]

It is vital to the health of our country that our educational programs reflect the diversity of our student bodies. We recognize and include our students when we reflect their experience in the curriculum. Place-based education gives us the opportunity to create content that is truly culturally responsive.

Through place-based education, teachers can shift the attention away from their own personal perspective to further explore the experience of their students. Children learn about issues relevant to them and build relationships with organizations that are working on similar topics. They will have the opportunity to examine the history of their particular place and gain more insights into local current events. Students and their communities are at the center of their learning, which will make each project unique to the needs and interests of that specific community.

"Soft" Skills

Traditional schooling does not prepare students for the world we live in today. Our colleges, universities, and places of work are not looking for young people who only know how to memorize facts, fill out worksheets, and work alone. Society is now in need of students with "soft" skills, many of which are also 21st-century skills.

The Partnership for 21st Century Learning has placed four learning and innovation skills at the heart of their "Framework for 21st Century Learning." Also known as the 4Cs, they are critical thinking, communication, collaboration, and creativity.[15]

Practicing these skills is a natural component of quality place-based education programming and is necessary in its implementation.

At its core, place-based education gives us a process through which we can reconnect with our community, our environment, and each other. In a 2013 interview with Bill Moyers, the writer, activist, and farmer Wendell Berry said, "We have the world to live in on the condition that we will take good care of it. And to take good care of it, we have to know it. And to know it and be willing to take care of it, we have to love it."[16]

There are many ways to know, love, and care for our world, from incorporating diverse perspectives to honoring the rural or urban nature of our environment to teaching our kids to treat each other and the places they live with kindness and compassion. Place-based education provides a way for us to bring our children more fully into the world while preparing them to be strong and capable stewards of their own future.

RESOURCES

Place-Based Education: Connecting Classrooms and Communities by David Sobel (2013) is a must-read for anyone just learning about place-based education. The short book is full of examples and suggestions.

Learning to Make Choices for the Future: Connecting Public Lands, Schools, and Communities through Place-Based Learning and Civic

Engagement is a valuable manual by Delia Clark (2008). Prepared by the Center for Place-Based Learning and Community Engagement and A Forest for Every Classroom, it offers a succinct introduction to place-based education, a how-to guide for creating partnerships, and lots of great tips and tools for project planning.

The Complete Guide to Service Learning: Proven, Practical Ways to Engage Students in Civil Responsibility, Academic Curriculum, and Social Action by Cathryn Berger Kaye (2010) offers a comprehensive explanation of service learning and its goals. The book also gives several concrete examples of how tie service-learning projects to all curricular subjects, complete with supporting resources.

"What is Place-Based Education and Why Does It Matter?" designed by Getting Smart in partnership with eduInnovation and Teton Science Schools, is the first publication in a three-part series aiming to define place-based education and help with its implementation. http://www.gettingsmart.com/wp-content/uploads/2017/02/What-is-Place-Based-Education-and-Why-Does-it-Matter-3.pdf

Getting Smart hosted a series of blog posts all about place-based education, most of them written by practicing teachers: http://www.gettingsmart.com/categories/series/place-based-education/

Last Child in the Woods by Richard Louv (2005) does a wonderful job of outlining the reasons why children now are more disconnected from each other and the places where they live as compared with the past.

NOTES

1. Ehrlich, Thomas. 2000. "The Definition of Civic Engagement," excerpts from *Civic Responsibility and Higher Education*. Westport, CT: Oryx Press. Accessed May 7, 2017. http://www.nytimes.com/ref/college/collegespecial2/coll_aascu_defi.html.

2. Clark, Delia. 2008. *Learning to Make Choices for the Future: Connecting Public Lands, Schools, and Communities through Place-Based Learning and Civic Engagement*. Woodstock, VT: National Park Service Conservation Study Institute.

3. Ibid.

4. Dewey, John. 1897. "My Pedagogic Creed." *School Journal* 54 (3): 77–80.

5. Louv, Richard. 2005. *Last Child in the Woods: Saving Our Children from Nature-Deficit Disorder*. Chapel Hill, NC: Algonquin.

6. Annenberg Public Policy Center. 2014. "Americans Know Surprisingly Little About Their Government, Survey Finds." Accessed May 7, 2017. http://www.annenbergpublicpolicycenter.org/americans-know-surprisingly-little-about-their-government-survey-finds.

7. Chumley, Cheryl K. 2014. "American Is an Oligarchy, Not a Democracy or Republic, University Study Finds." *Washington Times,* April 21. Accessed May 7, 2017. http://www.washingtontimes.com/news/2014/apr/21/americas-oligarchy-not-democracy-or-republic-unive.

8. Personal communication with author.

9. Cushman, Kathleen. 1997. "What Rural Schools Can Teach Urban Systems." *Challenge Journal* (The Journal of the Annenberg Challenge) 1 (2).

10. Sobel, David. 2013. *Place-Based Education: Connecting Classrooms and Communities*. Great Barrington, MA: Orion Society, 55–56.

11. Perkins, David N. 2016. "Lifeworthy Learning." *Educational Leadership* 73 (6): 12–17.

12. Mirel, Jeffrey, and Simona Goldin. 2012. "Alone in the Classroom: Why Teachers Are Too Isolated." *The Atlantic*, April 12. Accessed March 4, 2017. https://www.theatlantic.com/national/archive/2012/04/alone-in-the-classroom-why-teachers-are-too-isolated/255976.

13. United States Census Bureau. 2015. "New Census Bureau Report Analyzes U.S. Population Projections." Accessed March 24, 2017. https://www.census.gov/newsroom/press-releases/2015/cb15-tps16.html.

14. Holland, Jesse J. 2014. "U.S. Teachers Nowhere as Diverse as Their Students." Associated Press, March 4. Accessed March 24, 2017. http://thegrio.com/2014/05/04/us-teachers-nowhere-as-diverse-as-their-students.

15. P21: Partnership for 21st Century Learning. "Framework for 21st Century Learning." Accessed March 27, 2017. http://www.p21.org/our-work/p21-framework.

16. "Wendell Berry on His Hopes for Humanity." 2013, October 4. Interview with Bill Moyers on *Moyers & Company*, PBS. Accessed May 7, 2017. http://billmoyers.com/segment/wendell-berry-on-his-hopes-for-humanity.

CHAPTER 2

Mapping

 "If you don't know where you are, you don't know who you are."

—Wendell Berry (paraphrased by Wallace Stegner)[1]

Most of us have special places. For some, it may be a neighborhood or an entire city; for others it may be a park, a mountaintop, a lakeshore, or a shady spot in the backyard.

Special places play an equal or even bigger role in the lives of children. Think forts, treehouses, hidden trails, quiet corners, swimming holes, and playgrounds. These treasured locations are more than just places to spend time and have fun. Acknowledging and developing a child's connection to a place, whether it be a personal spot or a tract of land explored and "adopted" by the class, helps our students feel ownership and, in turn, more responsibility for the places where they live.

MAPPING AND GEOGRAPHY ARE CENTRAL IN THE PLACE-BASED CLASSROOM

One of the goals of place-based education is for students to know and better understand the land and communities around them. Reading and making maps help achieve this objective.

Maps ground us. As David Sobel writes in his book *Mapmaking with Children: A Sense of Place Education for the Elementary Years*,

"Maps are the clothespins that hitch our lives to our place."[2] By seeing and making pictures of where we are, we create a more intimate
relationship with the places where we live, work, and play. Mapping
encourages us to look closely at details and focus on the features that
make each place unique.

The ability to visualize where we are in space may be a disappearing
skill. With the advent of GPS, using a printed map seems foreign and
antiquated. When young people give all navigational tasks over to an
automated system, they are also giving up the information and skills
they need to be self-directed and confident in their environment. Using
maps helps make an imprint of the city and the land in our minds, and
the experience of finding our way—or perhaps to a larger extent losing
our way—can live in memories for a lifetime.

Geography is a national social studies standard. Many adults remember their geography lessons as exercises in memorization: name
the 50 states and their capitals, place all of the European countries
on a map, list the world's major rivers. Some adults still know songs
and other mnemonic devices to help retain all of the names and locations.

But knowing the name is knowing a place only on the most super-
ficial level. What are other reasons for studying maps? Dr. Charles
Gritzner, professor at South Dakota State University, explains the interdisciplinary nature of geography:

> Geography can be defined as the study of "What is where, why there,
> and why care." The "what," of course, does include capitals and rivers,
> but it involves so much more. In many respects, geography is the most
> complex of all disciplines. To be a good geographer: one must have a
> basic understanding of the fundamental elements of both the natural and
> social sciences; we must know: how the various elements interact to cre-
> ate the differences that exist from place to place, the names of various
> features, processes, and conditions, and finally (this is where geography
> comes in) we must know where all of this is located, why it's there, and
> of what importance it is to us and others.[3]

Using these guiding questions—"What is where, why there, and why
care?"—can help us better understand the intimate relationships be-

tween humans and the land. It also offers us an alternative way to view history and current events, using maps as a primary text. By looking at history spatially, instead of as an abstract timeline, the information becomes more concrete for students.

In urban areas, reading maps is a way to decipher the story of the city. Its buildings, streets, neighborhoods, monuments, and parks tell us who came before us, how they lived, what was important to them, what they considered beautiful, and how they treated each other. How did the land impact settlement? What industry was essential when the city began? How has it changed, and why? Students in rural areas can do the same examination on a smaller scale (or on a larger scale) by looking at an entire region of settlement. When we delve into a study of our place, whatever the focus may be, maps are an invaluable tool.

MAPMAKING TO BUILD CLASSROOM COMMUNITY

The more we know about where our students come from, the more potential there is for understanding and connection. When students make maps of the world as they know it, they are being asked to share a uniquely personal perspective. Honoring their experience lets kids know that they are important, and so are the places that they care about.

Teachers at the Cottonwood School of Civics and Science assign mapping projects at the beginning of the school year. One version of the assignment asks students to create a map of their neighborhood, highlighting all of the places that are of particular significance to the student. Another version asks students to make a map of their bedroom or another room that's important to them, including details that illustrate what makes this room significant. A third version moves away from the home and asks students to map a special place—perhaps a vacation spot, a relative's house, a city park, or some other place—that means a lot to the child (figure 2.1).

At the Cottonwood School, we have also engaged in personal mapping activities as a staff. We asked our teachers to remember and map

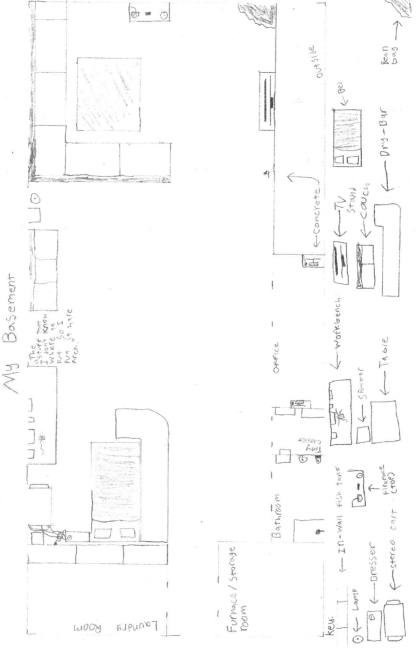

Figure 2.1. A 6th-grade student's map of his basement.

Sharing Personal Maps as a Way to Recognize Our Diverse Backgrounds and Promote Understanding

One of the simplest ways to foster compassion and understanding in our classrooms is to give students opportunities to share stories about their lives. By communicating and listening, students can break down stereotypes and see each other as real people. I've found particular success using the "neighborhood map." I typically assign this at the beginning of the school year as a get-to-know-you activity, but it can be done at any time.

I ask students to define and draw a map of their neighborhoods. Maybe it's the street where they live, the block, a section of town, or perhaps the entire town if it's small. I ask students to highlight and identify parts of their neighborhood that have significance for them. Sometimes these places go unnoticed by most people, but may have a special connection for the student. Maybe it's a place where they hang out with friends, the spot where they fell off a bike and broke an arm, or where they go to be alone. When their maps are finished (complete with title, color, and key), the students take turns presenting them to the class. Their presentations are followed by a time for respectful questions and comments.

In addition to students learning about each other, creating neighborhood maps also gives me a chance to know more about my students. I found out that one of my most troublesome 7th grade boys, who struggled in school and frequently acted out, loved exploring an urban creek by his house. He lit up when I asked him about the animals he'd seen there, which easily led to a writing assignment later. Another boy, whose social awkwardness often alienated him from his classmates, revealed that he had two neighborhoods because his parents had recently separated. This resulted in several compassionate connections from classmates who also knew what it was like to have divorced parents.

One of my most memorable experiences came when a boy who had been adopted from Liberia at age nine asked if he could draw his village. He spent days crafting his map and reliving memories from his early childhood. During his presentation, he told stories of playing soccer barefoot, learning how to cook from his grandmother over an open fire, and what it was like to run free all day with no adult supervision. His classmates asked many questions and learned a lot about what it is like to grow up in another culture.

Celebrating diverse perspectives is not just about recognizing other cultures and ethnicities. It is also about acknowledging that we all have rich and complex stories with varied pasts and personal struggles. The more we know about each other's lives, the easier it is to accept and understand.

Reprinted with permission of Teaching Tolerance, a project of the Southern Poverty Law Center.
http://www.tolerance.org/blog/mapping-out-get-know-you-project

special places from their childhood and share with the rest of the staff. The physical act of mapping led many teachers to reconnect with their childhood memories more directly than they had in years. When this reconnection happens, it helps us to remember the importance of places in a child's life and how long these experiences live in our imaginations.

CONSTRUCTING A SENSE OF PLACE IN LINE WITH A CHILD'S DEVELOPMENT

In his experience working with children, David Sobel has found a clear correlation between mapping and a child's developmental stage.[4] One thing he has observed is that the scale of a child's map changes with their age. When they are early elementary age, children tend to map small areas: their yard, a playground, a small park. As they get older, the borders of their maps broaden to include the neighborhood, the city, and then possibly on to state boundaries and beyond.

Sobel has also found that children's perspectives generally shift as they get older. He suggests that 3-D models are best for young students who are the most concrete thinkers, moving to more pictorial maps, and transitioning to the bird's-eye perspective when students are able to think more abstractly. Understanding how maps relate to our students' developmental stage is another way we can gain insight into the way they see the world around them.

One of the first things our students do in the fall at the Cottonwood School is to work together in small groups or as a whole class to map the school, city, or state. Each classroom has an assigned place to map that grows in scale according to age: Kindergarteners map their classroom, 1st and 2nd graders map the playground, 3rd graders map the school, 4th and 5th graders map local parks, 6th graders map the school's neighborhood, and 7th and 8th graders map the city of Portland or the state of Oregon.

There are several reasons why we decided to place a schoolwide emphasis on mapping at the beginning of the year. Primarily, the process grounds our students in where they live and learn, and promotes a sense of place.

In addition, the school-wide effort helps build community as all of the classrooms work to accomplish a common goal. The maps are displayed in school at the same time, so students, parents, and visitors can see the collective creation.

Mapping also requires many basic skills that are helpful to introduce and practice at the beginning of the school year, such as measurement, attention to detail, artistic layout, and presentation.

If a student attends our school for their entire elementary and middle school career, then they will have the complete experience of mapping their place paralleled with their own burgeoning understanding of the world.

Kindergarten, 1st, and 2nd Grades: Classroom and Playground

The kindergarten, 1st, and 2nd grade teachers follow a similar process when guiding their students through mapmaking. They begin by reading several picture books with maps in them and studying other examples of maps. Next, the students play with mapmaking by building maps out of wooden blocks, pattern blocks, and unifix cubes. Once they have had time to experiment with the different materials, the class works together to make a three-dimensional map of the classroom (fig. 2.2).

For kindergarteners, the classroom map is the end goal, so they take more time to prepare by choosing the parts of the classroom they think

Photo 2.1.   A classroom map built by kindergarteners.
Photo by Raina Janke

should be included and working in small groups to create sketches. They then use the sketches to build their assigned section out of recycled materials.

The 1st and 2nd graders use their class map to further explore the idea of spatial representation by playing games. The teacher or a student hides a penny in the classroom and then shows where it is hidden on the map with a sticker. Another student has to find the penny.[5] Building off this scaffolding, students go on to explore the playground, make sketches of key features, and construct a large map using recycled materials.

3rd Grade: School

In the past, our 3rd graders have approached their task of mapping the school with a unique perspective. They decided to make a sound map so that a visitor to our school would know what a typical day sounds like. To create this map, students worked in small groups as data collectors. Each group was assigned to a room where they went for a couple of listening sessions and wrote down all of the noises they heard. Students then worked in the classroom to turn all of those noise descriptions into onomatopoeias.

The final product was a very artistic representation. It may not have been perfectly to scale, but it was full of color and sound—perhaps a more accurate portrayal of our school than a basic blueprint!

4th, 5th, and 6th grades: Neighborhood

The 4th and 5th graders use the mapping challenge as a way to better explore parks in our neighborhood. Even if they have visited the parks before, this project gives them a reason to observe some features more closely. We have two parks in our neighborhood, allowing each class to become an expert on one of them.

As a complement to the mapmaking process, the 4th and 5th grade teachers ask students to write a paragraph comparing the two parks. This exercise pushes students to think more closely about the park features while meeting an important writing skill standard: writing to compare and contrast. Here is an example of a student's paragraph:

> Caruther's and Greenway are both close to my school. Greenway is long and skinny and only old people go there. Caruther's is shorter and fatter. It has a fountain and more kids go there. Caruther's has more plants than Greenway. Caruther's has chairs and tables by the fountain to sit. Greenway has a really cool concrete lounge chair which is really weird but strangely

comfortable. And Greenway has a nice beach. They are similar because they both have a nice grassy area.

In the end, the classes each create a scale drawing of their respective park. In order to ensure accuracy, the classes need to visit their location more than once to review their measurements. The students inevitably discover that one of the parks is significantly larger than the other, a fact that isn't as clear to them before they do this activity. They also find that one of the parks seems more intended for play, while the other appears to be designed for walking, biking, and sitting.

These observations impact how the students will view these parks specifically, but also parkland in general, in the future. Looking at the differences and similarities between parks can be a good entry into conversations about public land and planning. Why do we have parks in an urban area? Are they important? What should they be used for? How should they be maintained? Bringing our students' attention to these kinds of questions can inspire ownership and curiosity in our public spaces from an early age.

The 6th graders look at the buildings, streets, and other aspects of our neighborhood. After taking an initial tour of the neighborhood (which is really just a refresher for most students, especially if they have attended the school for several years already), students brainstorm a list of special features that could potentially be mapped. In 2016, the class came up with a list of over 40 features. Examples include food carts, restaurants, bike racks, fire hydrants, stoplights, benches, water fountains, graffiti and vandalism, and bioswales.

The class then breaks up into pairs or small groups of three. Each group is given the same map template, which includes streets and blocks. They work together to fill in the street names and choose what they will be mapping. Data collection requires a couple more walks through the neighborhood. Lastly, the groups design a map that visually incorporates aspects of the theme. They need to think about the artistic border, a cartouche, a title, symbols, and a color scheme that all reflect the mapped feature.

The final products are graded not just on accuracy, but also on beauty and creativity. One recent group's map of fire hydrants was titled "K9 Restroom Map." The border consisted of long dogs with wagging tails (figure 2.3). The title for the bike rack map was "Bane of the Bike Thieves," and the center of the compass rose was a bike wheel. The compass rose for "Mobile Eats of the South Waterfront" was a food cart with spikes coming out of it.

These neighborhood maps not only encourage our students to look more closely at places they have passed by dozens of times; they can also bring the community's attention to places they never noticed or thought about. Displaying these maps in the school or in another neighborhood venue is a great way to get people thinking and talking about community features. It can also lead to more questions: Why do we have bike racks on certain streets, but not others? Why are fire hydrants located where they are? Why doesn't this intersection have a stoplight? Why are there no green spaces in this area? Again, mapping serves as a way to spatially organize valuable observations and facts about the world around us.

7th and 8th Grades: City, State, and World

In 7th and 8th grades, maps illustrate answers to questions that students have about their city and state, alternating between the two every other year. The process for looking at a city and a state is similar, but for the purposes of explanation, we will look at the city assignment.

Students begin by sketching maps of Portland based on memory. Some students base maps on their favorite places, whereas others use their route to school. It is interesting to see how much or how little students know about their city and how much of their knowledge is concentrated in their local neighborhood or district.

Next, students receive an outline of Portland city boundaries. They learn where the borders are for the five distinct sections: Northwest, Northeast, North, Southeast, and Southwest. Students are asked to include major bodies of water and transportation routes. Then the teacher asks each student to identify one place in each district that is special or memorable to them: a restaurant, museum, park, friend's house . . . someplace where they have been that is personally significant to them.

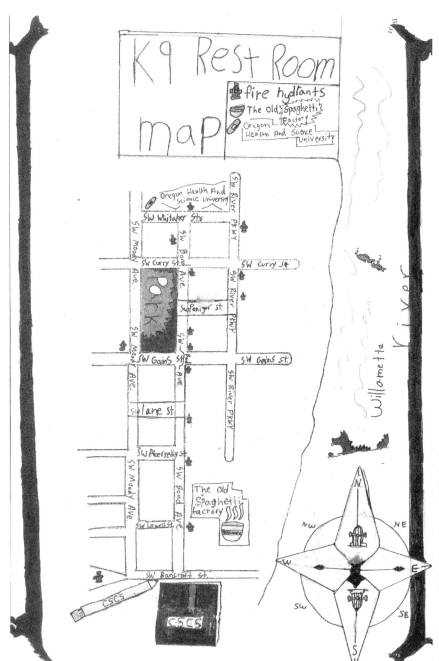

Figure 2.2. Neighborhood map of fire hydrants.

Last, the class explores statistical data about Portland and chooses one data set to map citywide. Examples of maps from a recent year included population, temperature levels during a heat wave, city parks, and Starbucks locations (photo 2.2).

Just as with other the other mapping projects, this last layer of information can lead to many questions about the city. Why do certain areas have more people than others? Why is one area so hot when another is 10 degrees cooler? Why is there a Starbucks on every corner? Exploring possible answers to these questions can serve as a perfect segue into studies in environmental science, local history, economics, sociology, and a number of other topics.

Our 7th and 8th grade social studies curriculum goes on to look more closely at national history and global geography. Completing this project at the beginning of the year is a perfect way for students to gain familiarity with maps and cartography skills.

ILLUSTRATING INJUSTICE AND AREAS OF CONCERN

Maps can be both powerful and persuasive. Teachers can use maps to teach about social injustices of the past and create maps that highlight present-day concerns.

When studying Portland's history, our 6th graders learn that the city's banks practiced redlining with the intention of segregating neighborhoods and keeping black homeowners in one part of town. When students look at demographic maps from the 1940s and 1950s, it is clear where the red lines fell.

Portland was once home to a bustling Japantown, but after FDR's Executive Order 9066 forcibly relocated Japanese Americans to detention camps, most residents never returned to that part of the city. The consequences of this executive action are clear when students look at demographic maps contrasting prewar and postwar statistics.

By comparing demographic maps and focusing on race and ethnicity, students can also track how urban development and gentrification have created an ongoing migration of people, first to the center of the city and now to the outskirts. It is also clear how the African American community, which was once mostly enclosed in a small section of the city, has moved farther east and dispersed. Similar observations could

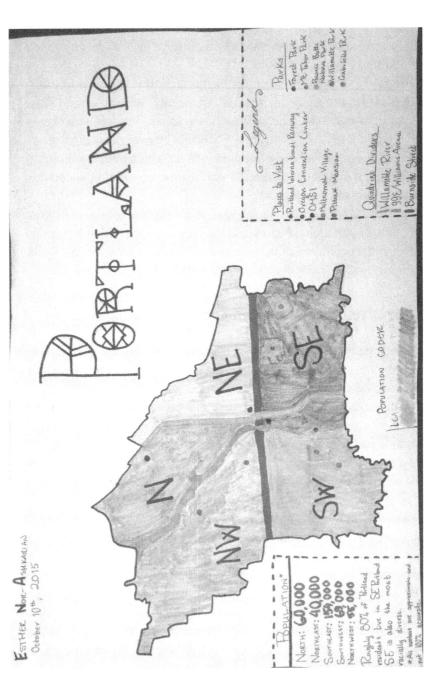

Photo 2.2. *An 8th grader's map of Portland, showing both population and special places.*
Photo by author

be made about a large percentage of Asian Americans who no longer live in Portland's historic Chinatown.

Making maps can also be a tool for students who are working to make policy change. As a model, it has proven to be a successful strategy by Portland's Regional Equity Atlas. The website offers this definition:

> An equity atlas is a tool that enables us to understand how well different neighborhoods and populations are able to access the resources and opportunities necessary for meeting their basic needs and advancing their health and well-being. By providing a visual depiction of disparities, equity atlases can play a powerful role in guiding policy, planning, and strategic investments to create more equitable communities.[6]

The Equity Atlas even provides guides and tutorials to help people make their own maps. Creating a map for the Atlas could be a great possibility for a student project, or classrooms can use mapping to support other ongoing efforts.

Maps and mapmaking serve as indispensable tools to incorporate social justice into the curriculum, especially as our students are able to analyze data and suggest policy changes of their own.

MAPPING TO TAKE INVENTORY AND IMAGINE POSSIBILITY

We can also use maps to imagine improvements and change in the places where we live and work.

We once led our middle schoolers through a city design project as part of our civics curriculum. The process began with students making maps of their own neighborhoods, highlighting the areas that are most special and important to them and their families. Once students made and shared these neighborhood maps, we asked students to journal about this question: "If you could change one thing about your neighborhood to make it better, what would you change?"

After reflecting and writing on this prompt, students went back into their maps and added potential improvement sites or features. This exercise allowed students to imagine the possibility of positive change in their neighborhood and placed the students in the position of problem-solvers and changemakers. Even though this role was imaginary, the process has the ability to give students a tangible sense of empowerment.

In the next stage, students formed small groups to work together as city planners. Their task was to make a plan for a city that would most effectively meet the needs of its populace. Each group was given the same base map for their city, which included a river, a bay, and mountains. The groups were also given different sets of demographics describing the makeup of their city's population, including ethnic groups, income, education, industry, and age.

Obviously, this exercise is far from realistic. No planner builds a city from scratch already knowing the populace's demographics. But the project helped students to think more deeply about the layout of a city and how services can best meet the needs of the people. How will this look different according to different demographics? What impact does industry have on how a city looks? What services should every city provide? How can we be more involved in making our city work for everyone?

Going through this process can also help students become more skilled at analyzing information on other maps as they encounter them throughout the year. Inviting a city planner into the classroom adds another level of learning about how our cities operate and plan for the future.

The *Healthy Neighborhoods, Healthy Kids Guide* published by Shelburne Farms' Sustainable Schools Project outlines a similar lesson in their curriculum as preparation for action. The guide is designed to help students identify quality of life indicators in their neighborhood, conduct an inventory, and plan a service project. In the scaffolding stages, students read, write, and talk about the idea of "place" and locations that are special to them. They also map their own neighborhood, their route to school, and the school neighborhood.

Before they delve into investigating quality of life indicator features, the guide asks students to create maps of their ideal neighborhoods. When sharing their maps, the teacher helps students identify the features that make the neighborhood comfortable and desirable. The class lists these feature, ideally grouping them in categories such as Sidewalks and Paths, Access to Transit, Calm Traffic, Greenspace, Mixed Use, and Neighbors. This exercise helps students to understand and define features of healthy neighborhoods, which they can then apply to a real-life assessment.[7]

MAPPING ALSO TEACHES OTHER SKILLS

Mapping is a truly interdisciplinary undertaking. As with most place-based projects, you can connect the work to several different curricular topics.

- Geography and Orienteering: Reading and making maps teaches students concepts such as cardinal directions, latitude and longitude, basic landforms, and elements of a map. This information will be valuable when studying history, science, current events, statistics, and other subjects. Plus, orienteering skills will be useful throughout life.
- Science/Ecological Studies: Mapmaking can assist students in many activities such as documenting a vegetation plot or mapping animal signs. Maps can accompany data collection efforts; our teachers have used them when gathering information about tree species in the neighborhood or the number of banana slugs along a forest hike.

    Students can also make maps to imagine a place through the eyes of a specific animal. For example, they could show a park from the perspective of a squirrel or a coyote to learn about habitat, diet, and behavior. What would be an important landmark for the animal? What about their points of interest and transportation trails? This activity can easily overlap with writing descriptive narratives about the animals or from their points of view.
- Art: From ancient scrolls to modern art pieces, maps can be beautiful and creative. When making maps with children, show them examples of lots of different maps and draw their attention to elements such as the cartouche, the border, the compass rose, the pictorial representations, color schemes, and other flourishes like sea monsters in the ocean. The book *Map Art Lab: 52 Exciting Map Explorations in Mapmaking, Imagination, and Travel* by Jill K. Berry and Linden McNeilly outlines some great mini-lessons

on how to thoughtfully create each element of a map. Teachers can set a standard for creativity by adding design expectations to rubrics and scoring tools.

- Language Arts: As we saw with the 4th and 5th grade neighborhood park mapping project, mapmaking can serve as a wonderful inspiration for writing. Once students have a comprehensive drawing of a place, writing can become much easier. Details on maps can readily transfer into details in a written piece. This can be especially powerful when students write about their special places. We have seen reluctant writers talk animatedly about their special place maps and then transition that excited energy into rich written pieces.

  Students can also write about maps they didn't make, but that they have had time to study. Maps that contain statistical information can generate lots of questions, which in turn can turn into written hypotheses or research papers.

  Making maps after reading can help deepen reading comprehension. Mapping the setting of a novel demands that students pay close attention to written details. Asking students to map natural processes such as the water cycle or wind currents can also strengthen understanding of science texts.

- Math: Making maps inherently requires multiple math skills, especially ratio and measurement. Most teachers preface a mapmaking project with a lesson on scale and proportion, no matter what grade level. Using the grid method for enlarging drawings also serves as a lesson in art.

  Displaying data on maps is a helpful extension of statistics. Transferring information from a datasheet to a map makes it more concrete and therefore more accessible. Once students see that the numbers apply to the places where they live, the information will naturally feel more relevant.

Integrating maps and mapmaking into a curriculum grounds any topic within a particular place. Students gain familiarity with locations while also thinking more carefully about why things are where they are. But most important, we can guide our students to ask themselves "Why care?" when reading and making maps. It is within this question and its many answers that we can see more clearly where we come from and where we are going.

RESOURCES

Mapmaking with Children: Sense of Place Education for the Elementary Years by David Sobel (1998) is the primary resource for teachers looking to integrate mapmaking into a developmentally appropriate, place-based curriculum. The book contains several examples and practical ideas.

Map Art Lab: 52 Exciting Map Explorations in Mapmaking, Imagination, and Travel by Jill K. Berry and Linden McNeilly (2014) is a teacher's guide to connecting mapmaking and art. It includes several lessons on the different components of a map and how to make them beautiful.

Healthy Neighborhood, Healthy Kids Guide, published by Shelburne Farms' Sustainable Schools Project (2015), uses neighborhood mapping as a jumping off point for civic action.

My Place by Nadia Wheatley and Donna Rawlins (2008) follows the history of an Australian town over hundreds of years through the eyes of all of the different children who claimed it as their own. Each historical period includes a short written narrative and a hand-drawn map from the child's perspective. A great tool to explore mapping and diverse perspectives with older children.

Me on the Map is a picture book written by Joan Sweeney and illustrated by Annette Cable (1996). It juxtaposes drawings of the narrator's different places (bedroom, house, town, state, etc.) with maps of that place. A good introduction to representational mapmaking.

Where Do I Live?, written by Neil Chesanow and illustrated by Ann Iosa (1995), is not a book of maps, but it is a good tool to help teachers "zoom out" through the different layers of a locale. The first page starts with the concept of a bedroom, the next page is about the house, the next is about land, then street, neighborhood, town, etc. Simple descriptive sentences accompany each page.

Mapping Penny's World by Loreen Leedy (2000) is an introduction to mapping components through the narration of Lisa, who has received a mapping assignment at school. Her Boston terrier, Penny, plays a central role in Lisa's maps. This book can be a helpful example when exploring diverse perspectives and when making maps from the point of view of animals.

My Map Book by Sarah Fanelli (1995) is a fun, colorful collection of maps that introduce children to a world of mapmaking possibilities. Examples include a map of a dog, a heart, and a day.

Everything Sings: Maps for a Narrative Atlas by Denis Wood (2010) is an intriguing example of how one place can be viewed through multiple lenses. The book contains dozens of maps all of one neighborhood, but each with a different focus. Data sets include sidewalk graffiti, wind chimes, and jack-o'-lanterns.

A Map of the World According to Illustrators and Storytellers, edited by Antonis Antoniou, Robert Klanten, Sven Ehmann, and Hendrik Hellige (2013), is a collection of beautifully designed maps from around the world. It's a great book to have in the classroom for students to thumb through for inspiration.

NOTES

1. Stegner, Wallace. 1992. "The Sense of Place." In *Where the Bluebird Sings to the Lemonade Springs: Living and Writing in the West*, 199–206. New York: Random House.

2. Sobel, David. 1998. *Mapmaking with Children: Sense of Place Education for the Elementary Years*. Portsmouth, NH: Heinemann, 3.

3. Baskerville, Brian. 2013. "Becoming Geographers: An Interview about Geography with Geographer Dr. Charles Gritzner." *About.com*. Accessed

May 8, 2017. http://geography.about.com/od/historyofgeography/fl/Becoming
-Geographers.htm

4. Sobel, *Mapmaking with Children*, 10–23.

5. Sobel, *Mapmaking with Children*, 29–32.

6. Regional Equity Atlas: Geography of Opportunity. "Equity Atlas On-line Toolkit." Accessed May 10, 2017. http://regionalequityatlas.org/toolkit/equity-atlas-toolkit-overview.

7. Tillman, Tiffany. 2015. "Ideal Neighborhood Mapping." In *Healthy Neighborhoods, Healthy Kids Guide*, eds. Ryan Morra, Holly Brough, and Jen Cirillo. Shelburne, VT: Shelburne Farms' Sustainable Schools Project, 41–43.

CHAPTER 3

Community Science

Sustainability is built on the foundations of ecology and the understanding that everything in a community is interconnected and reliant on other parts. According to David Orr, "'Ecological sustainability' . . . recognizes humankind as part of nature, that there are limits to growth and carrying capacity and that nature should be regarded as a model for the design of housing, cities, neighborhoods, technologies and regional economies."[1]

This approach offers an especially useful framework for science education by integrating scientific thinking with social and economic studies. Projects require students to collaborate, solve problems, and think creatively.[2]

Science connects to community in many ways. Students can become experts in important topics such as natural resources or public health. Or they can collect data for local agencies. Kids can even influence public policy through research and presentations. As with all place-based projects, the common thread is connecting curricular content to the community.

STUDENTS AS TEACHERS

In order to create a sustainable future, we need citizens with a solid science education. If we want cities that do little harm to the ecosystem and provide a healthy environment for their populace, we especially need to know earth science. In an urban area this starts with knowing the infrastructure. As students learn more about how their city works, their knowledge becomes a public resource. This gives us the opportunity to design projects in which students teach other citizens pertinent information about the community they share.

Ancient Walls Geology Quest

The area around Portland has a very rich geological history and even has active volcanos. But when we assigned the study of rocks and minerals to the 4th and 5th grade, teachers Susan Hathaway and Katie Holder looked for a way to teach geology without having to leave the city.

We found that a local organization, the Geological Society of the Oregon Country (GSOC), offers a guided tour to teach about all of the different rocks found in the buildings of downtown Portland. The tour, however, is geared toward adults.

We approached the GSOC to see if they would be interested in a kid-friendly, self-guided version of the tour that they could then distribute to families or schools. The organization responded very favorably and even offered the teachers a private tour in order to convey information and answer content questions.

On the tour we learned that an urban environment can tell a fascinating geologic story. In the floor of a downtown mall we saw ancient squid and starfish fossils. In the outside walls of other buildings we discovered: stone from the roots of a 1.8-billion-year-old compressed Minnesota mountain, the same Italian marble that Michelangelo used to carve David, and other rocks from France, Germany, India, California, and Indiana. We found that our city is alive with many examples of sedimentary, igneous, and metamorphic rock.

Over the course of a trimester, the 4th and 5th grade students visited numerous locations downtown. They worked in small groups to research and write about specific buildings or other locations (photo 3.1). At the same time, the teachers taught geology lessons in the classroom to help students become experts on different rock types.

The culminating product was a fun, educational scavenger hunt called a "quest." A quest moves readers through an area using written clues and a map. Once the quester (the person following the clues) finds a location, the text gives educational facts about that spot. There

Photo 3.1.   Getting a closer look at the geology of downtown Portland.
Photo by Erin Wagner

is also an embedded puzzle that the quester solves by the end in order to find a treasure box. The box contains even more information about the sites, a sign-in book, and a stamp.

Once the students finished crafting all aspects of the quest—which included text, illustrations of the locations, a map, a treasure box, handmade sign-in books, and a stamp—and had tested it out and made important edits, we organized a celebration at a small downtown museum where the treasure box now resides. During the celebration, students talked about their process, read excerpts from the quest, and officially handed it over to a representative from the GSOC. Parents and the press were also invited.

Teacher Susan Hathaway comments that creating this quest was a great way to connect the topic of geology to the city where she lives. Completing this project changed the way she views downtown; many of the buildings have a new meaning and context. Now when students go to Central Library, the theater, or the shopping mall with their families, they have an extra layer of connection and understanding of these places.[3]

The human-made environment of a city offers many more opportunities for teaching about the earth and its resources. Exploring building materials can inspire units about geology, but can also spark inquiries into the practice of mining, international trade, architecture, and the human history of dwellings. What building materials and practices are most sustainable? Which are the least sustainable? Unpacking a city's infrastructure can lead to the study of many more natural resources, such as energy and water, and how we use them.

The City's Water System

There is a Chinese saying: "When you drink water, think of its source." In the developed world, it is easy for us to forget about the value and importance of clean water. Drinking, cooking, and bathing are usually just a faucet-turn away. But even in urban areas, there are often events that give us pause and force us to consider where our water comes from and how it gets to us.

Concerns about water have made headlines in Portland several times in recent years. The city has issued drinking water bans because of E. coli contamination and cryptosporidium.[4] High lead content has forced many of the public schools in the city to send daily loads of bottled drinking water to classrooms.[5] Battles rage over adding fluoride to our water when the topic comes up for voter input.[6] One of our local reservoirs was even drained when a drunken resident urinated into it.[7]

Talking, thinking, and making informed choices about public water is something every city resident should be able to do. Recent national headlines, such as the lead crisis in Flint, Michigan, also clearly connect the topic to equity, access, and social justice. Introducing our students to these issues forces them to think deeper about a resource they might otherwise take for granted.

Teacher Chris Wyland knew that his 7th and 8th grade students needed to see the city's water system firsthand in order to become experts. We arranged a tour through the Portland Water Bureau for the classes to visit Bull Run, the source of Portland's drinking water. This large reservoir is highly protected, and people can see it only on tours led by the bureau. It is provocative for students to travel the hour and a half it takes to drive to Bull Run and imagine how much work goes into maintaining all those miles of pipes.

We continued our partnership with the water bureau by visiting one of its operational facilities in the city. Students learned about water meters, groundwater, water testing, and water pressure, giving them more information about all of the work that goes into guaranteeing clean drinking water for the citizens of Portland.

To learn about the other end of the system, students toured a sewer treatment plant (photo 3.2). They had a behind-the-scenes look at the mechanical, chemical, and microbiological regimen that water goes through before it is released back into waterways and rivers. An educator from Portland's Bureau of Environmental Services also came into the class to present a program called "After the Flush," which guided students through the water treatment process.

To supplement the hands-on learning, teachers gave a refresher on the water cycle and led discussions on the world's drinking supply and water crises in other counties. The class also imagined what it was like for the first humans in Portland to find a suitable drinking source. Students then chose topics to research further, such as aquifers, water rights, hydroelectric power, or another local or global issue related to water.

The students augmented what they had learned over the trimester by delving deeper into their chosen topic. Then they generated and implemented an action plan to somehow impact their topic positively.

Photo 3.2. A visit to a waste water treatment plant.
Photo by Chris Wyland

Lastly, they created a website to raise awareness and document their own process and efforts. A community volunteer helped students to develop their websites while teachers supported the students as they researched and created content.

To celebrate the unit, students shared their knowledge with the community through a science fair format. Other students, parents, and interested

Connecting Place-Based Science to Social and Ecological Justice

by Chris Wyland
Middle School Science Teacher
The Cottonwood School of Civics and Science

My middle school students used their knowledge of Portland's water system as a foundation for exploring connections between social justice and water. My co-teacher Emily Conner and I introduced possible topics, ranging from disputes over Lake Chad in Africa to local water rights and policies. In small groups, students identified topics they felt passionate about and worked to become experts. After students performed extensive background research on the issue, each group selected one aspect of their topic where they could create some sort of change; this became their action plan.

One such group of students selected the Standing Rock Nation protest against the Dakota Access Pipeline. This protest was happening in full swing at the time of our water unit. In their research and through network connections within the school, this group met and interviewed a local resident who went to Standing Rock to build housing for women and children. The students invited this activist into the classroom.

When speaking to the class, the activist started off by honoring the Chinook people who once lived on the land our school is currently occupying. This introduction completely changed the perspective of many of my students, and it forced everyone to reconsider an idea we take for granted: that we own the land we live on legally and fairly.

This speaker then went on to explain how many Native Americans hold water as sacred. It is considered to be a part of the human existence, and thus to pollute the water source is to pollute one's own body. There was an authentic dialogue between the guest speaker and students while they wrestled with this different way of regarding water. Only through the passion and facilitation of the students who tackled this topic was this new perspective able to be introduced in the classroom.

Promoting connections to social and ecological justice within my science curriculum inspired a deeper, more meaningful experience for my middle school students. In turn, they were able to teach others. They scheduled time to give presentations about the Standing Rock protest in each of the classrooms within the building, as well as raise awareness through a poster campaign. This group did a great job of treating a potentially controversial topic with respect and dignity. This was possible because they had the time and motivation to carefully examine a complicated issue that might be ignored in a traditional science classroom.

community members attended. In this environment, students transformed from pupils to experts. The community members expressed astonishment at the level of student knowledge and were particularly impressed by their ability to modulate content for adults versus kindergarteners. The students even surprised themselves with how much they knew and how confidently they could speak on their topics. They admitted that although the project was hard work, the celebration made it all worthwhile.

"DOING SCIENCE" AND THE NEW STANDARDS

For the past 150 years, scientific research has been the domain of professional scientists. Before that, almost all inquiries were carried out by average citizens who were simply curious. Since the 1990s, nonprofessionals have advocated to participate in data collection and research.[8] This form of participation, coined "citizen science," is part of what the philosopher Paul Feyerabend called the "democratization of science."[9]

Nonprofit organizations lead the effort to empower curious citizens. The Audubon Society has held its Christmas Day Bird Count since 1900. In the 1970s, butterfly count programs allowed the general public to provide data. Project FeederWatch out of Cornell Lab of Ornithology has been around since the mid-1970s and gives birdwatchers an opportunity to contribute data to published research.[10]

In recent years, more organizations have set up programs that welcome contributions from schools and students. *Scientific American* has even dedicated a section of its website to different citizen science programs around the country. These programs offer students an amazing opportunity to "do real science." In other words, student work has a relevant outcome while students make a substantive impact and witness how concepts are interwoven into everyday life.

The optimal way to learn science is to be a scientist. The designers of the Next Generation Science Standards (NGSS) agree. These new standards have shifted the learning focus from straight content to a combination of core ideas and practices. Practices, described as the coordination of both knowledge and skill, are employed when students conduct authentic research. According to the NGSS, "The actual doing of science or engineering can also pique students' curiosity, capture their interest, and motivate their continued study."[11]

Instead of listing facts that students need to memorize, the NGSS asks that students show understanding through practice. For example, two of the middle school "earth systems" standards state:

Students who demonstrate understanding can:

- Develop a model to describe the cycling of Earth's materials and the flow of energy that drives this process.
- Construct a scientific explanation based on evidence for how the uneven distributions of Earth's mineral, energy, and groundwater resources are the result of past and current geoscience processes.[12]

The active language used in these standards makes them easily applicable to a variety project-based and place-based units. Many skills applied in place-based projects are identified in the NGSS as core practices, such as data collection, analysis, and experiment conduction.

Additionally, cross-curricular connections are clear. Communicating information is a highlighted skill: "A major practice of science is thus the communication of ideas and the results of inquiry—orally, in writing, with the use of tables, diagrams, graphs, and equations, and by engaging in extended discussions with scientific peers."[13]

Additionally, skills in reading and analyzing nonfiction texts, another crossover into language arts, are necessary.

As evidenced by the NGSS, both educators and professionals increasingly recognize the need for school to be more interdisciplinary.

Place-based projects are a perfect vehicle for this type of advanced learning. Many projects incorporate real-world examples of basic math concepts like measurement, statistics, and percentages. Additionally, an integrated science unit easily includes social studies topics such as policy-making, current events, and the history of urban development.

CITIZEN SCIENCE IN ACTION

The following projects incorporate citizen science and easily connect to the NGSS. In all of these cases, the teacher found ways to link important instructional content to a real community need.

Urban Forestry

When we began designing a unit on forestry, we first looked to the Cascade Mountains, an hour or more east of the city. But since transportation is always an issue, our 7th and 8th grade science teacher Chris Wyland decided to stay close to home.

We found that the city of Portland has an Urban Forestry Department that manages 236,000 urban street trees and 1.2 million park trees. According to the "Portland Plan," a goal-based action plan for the future development of Portland, our city currently has a tree canopy that covers 26 percent of the city. Because of the many ways trees benefit an environment, the city has made tree planting and maintenance a priority. The goal is to establish a canopy over the next several years that covers 33 percent. Thousands of trees have been planted in Portland as a joint effort between the city, the Bureau of Environmental Services, a nonprofit called Friends of Trees, and other organizations.[14]

The Urban Forestry's Tree Inventory Project offers an avenue for community members to help with tree management in the neighborhoods where they live. Volunteers are trained to accurately measure and assess street trees. The data collected by the volunteers is then analyzed at an annual "Tree Summit" held every November. During the summit, each participating neighborhood puts together a development plan for their trees, including recommendations for planting new ones.

Our school's neighborhood is fairly new and many of the trees are young. The canopy is still years away. It is also one of the neighborhoods that had not been officially inventoried, giving us a perfect opportunity. In order to complete the inventory, students needed to know how to identify several different species and learn technical forestry terms like DBH (diameter at breast height). They needed to log neat, precise data and work in small fieldwork groups independent from the class as a whole (photo 3.3).

After collecting data, students examined the results and brainstormed questions. Small groups focused on one particular data set, such as overall health and age of trees and range of species. They made posters that highlighted their topic and created presentations including questions and recommendations for the Urban Forestry Department. They also made recommendations on what kinds of trees should be planted in the empty spaces available.

Photo 3.3.   Student measuring the diameter of an Oregon white oak.
Photo by author

At the end of the trimester, the class held their own mini "tree summit" attended by a representative from the city. The visitor listened graciously but also challenged students if their thinking was too simplistic or if they ignored an important piece of information. Students needed to utilize several of the NGSS "practices" asked of middle schoolers: analyzing and interpreting data, constructing explanations and designing solutions, and engaging in argument from evidence. Written and oral communication played an essential role.

The urban tree project is an example of how an authentic audience can naturally raise expectations for student work. It is also a great example of how students can get involved in a local effort to maintain and protect a natural resource.

Portland Urban Coyote Project

Coyotes have attracted a lot of attention in the press and social media, although it is clear that they have lived in our city and neighborhoods for a very long time. When the 4th and 5th grade teachers chose an urban animal to study, coyotes appeared to be a great option, partly because of the controversy surrounding them.

Many people view coyotes as villains. They are considered cat killers, wild animals that are dangerous to us. Coyote sightings are often posted on Portland neighborhood social media sites under the Crime and Safety section.

The Portland Urban Coyote Project (PUCP) has emerged as a collaboration between the Audubon Society and a group of researchers in the geography department of Portland State University. It allows the general public to participate in mapping coyote sightings throughout the metropolitan area. Their website, PortlandCoyote.com, includes an interactive map showing all the places where sightings have occurred, categorized by year and time of day.

PUCP's website includes an online tutorial for people to learn more about coyotes. After taking the tutorial, a user will know more about coyote biology, their history in Portland, how to identify them and their signs, and how to coexist with the animals in an urban area. The format and content are incredibly accessible, and the fact that it is also interactive makes it a perfect teaching tool for elementary school children.

The website was a primary resource as students researched coyote biology and looked specifically at how the animals live in urban areas. Teachers Susan Hathaway and Courtney Miller also checked out books from the public library about coyotes, many of which contained chapters about urban living.

Next, the classrooms hosted the leader of PUCP, who brought in coyote artifacts (such as a skull) and talked with students about the effort to educate the public (such as conveying the fact that cats make up only 1 to 2 percent of an urban coyote's diet).

After that initial visit, the class discussed ways students could help the Coyote Project with its mission and website. One group wrote a song, another group created informational flyers to post in neighborhoods, and yet another wrote and performed a skit to teach kindergarten through 3rd graders what to do when confronted with a coyote. A few students also made comic strips to teach other kids how to keep coyotes away from their houses. These comics were handed out to the audience members after the skit (figure 3.1).

The Coyote Project representative visited the class toward the end of the trimester to see students work and give feedback. As a last step, teachers sent material to the Coyote Project to be included on its website.

Not only did students learn more than the average citizen about a common urban animal, but they were also able to take their newfound knowledge and turn it into action. It is clear to kids that they are not just learning ecology and practicing language arts for the sake of school; their education can be immediately applied to current efforts in the city where they live.

Water Quality

When the 7th and 8th grade students studied the water cycle and watersheds, science teacher Paul Banta found a way for them to collect useful data while also taking full advantage of Portland's natural areas. Most of the original waterways in the city have been forced underground into culverts, but one creek has been protected and runs mostly aboveground through the west hills and down to the Willamette River.

Figure 3.1. A comic strip offers advice (using humor) on how to co-exist with urban coyotes.

Tryon Creek even has its own state park, one of the only state parks found within the boundaries of an Oregon city.

After refreshing their knowledge of the water cycle, students learned more about watersheds, erosion, and pollution coupled with weekly visits to Tryon Creek. On the first visit, students learned how to conduct water quality tests: pH, turbidity, temperature, and dissolved oxygen. After that, they worked in trios to collect and record the data over the course of the fall at different points along the creek. On one visit, we ran into a group of college students who were conducting the same exact tests. Our 7th and 8th grade students immediately made the connection that they were doing real, adult work, which served as additional motivation.

Toward the end of the trimester, students analyzed their data and, as with the urban forestry unit, created presentations to give information and offer recommendations to a group of scientists who were involved with managing the creek. The final presentation resembled a science fair, except it focused on one topic and was geared toward making real contributions to the local research community.

In cooperation with the NGSS, students demonstrated understanding by "Construct[ing] an argument supported by evidence for how increases in human population and per-capita consumption of natural resources impact Earth's systems."[15] Students also analyzed and interpreted data, constructed explanations, and designed solutions—all desired practices according to NGSS.

Water quality testing is an easy way to get students out of the classroom and "doing" science. There are agencies and organizations within most communities that value data taken by students, and there may be online citizen science site collecting results. Water quality testing is also a great way to see chemistry in action and view firsthand how rivers and streams are affected by other conditions in an ecosystem.

INFORMING PUBLIC POLICY

Analyzing data and offering recommendations to scientists and agency representatives can be one goal of a place-based science unit. It is also vital that our kids see how scientific research informs public policy.

This is especially poignant now that data is being challenged by politicians when it does not support their agendas. Along the way, there may be opportunities for students to get involved in making policy or informing the public about a little-known law.

The Problem of Pet Waste

When our 7th and 8th graders set out to identify problems in our neighborhood, they decided to survey local residents and record their own observations. After considering a host of issues, the classes settled on the problem of dog waste.

It may sound like a small problem, but students decided that it was large enough to affect both quality of life in the area and ecological health. The streets smelled so rancid that whenever the kindergarteners walked to the local park they would chant, "Dog Poop City! Dog Poop City!" Anyone walking on the sidewalk had to constantly check their path (and hold their nose) to make sure their foot didn't land in a pile of waste. And to boot, our neighborhood is adjacent to the Willamette River, making rain runoff all the more toxic.

The students knew they wanted to find a solution to this problem, but they would most likely need help from the city government in terms of communication and enforcement. In order to capture the city government's attention, they would need a good argument, which meant research and evidence.

Students worked in teams to collect data and conduct research. One team walked around the neighborhood and mapped all the piles of pet waste they could find. In one day, they found 75 piles within a six-block radius. Another team researched the environmental toxins in dog poop and their effect on water quality and human health. Another group looked into the current laws surrounding pet waste in Portland, while yet another group looked into laws in other cities and countries.

With data and research in hand, students discussed the best solution to the problem. They decided that the approach should be twofold: a heavier penalty and increased education. They drafted a proposal to make the fine for dog owners higher. They also recommended that the city do more to teach about the dangers of improperly disposed dog feces. The class sent their written proposal, data findings, and a petition to the commissioner in charge of city parks.

Within a couple of weeks, they got a response. The commissioner invited the class to city hall to present to him directly. A few weeks later, students received a thank you letter from him for their work and concern. He also informed them that the parks department was about to launch a city-wide pet owner education campaign called "Petiquette" and told them that their recommendations were taken into consideration during the program's development. The students felt an amazing sense of empowerment because their work and actions led to real change.

Through this process, students also learned that solutions that seem simple are much more complex once you dig below the surface. For example, they quickly turned to enforcement as a solution but found through interviewing the city that there is only one park ranger assigned to all of the parks in our region, making enforcement nearly impossible. City officials also pointed out that most owners will pick up after their dog if someone is watching, making enforcement all the more difficult. Students decided to include education as part of their plan, which was apparently in line with the city's thinking as well. Civic problems can rarely be addressed with a "quick fix."

Plastic Bag Ban

In 2011, the Portland newspapers were abuzz with the possibility of a plastic bag ban in major grocery and department stores. Our 4th and 5th grade teacher, Lisa Colombo, turned this current event into an opportunity to study pollution, waste, and recycling while making the issue more relevant for her students.

She started the unit with a hands-on project. The class conducted a trash audit for the entire school. Trash audits are a perfect first service-learning project for any teacher. They are local, self-contained, easy to organize, and results-oriented, and they perform a real service to the school.

Essentially, the process requires students to collect trash and recycling cans from all of the rooms in the school, sort through the contents, record data, weigh waste, and write reports for each room based on the findings. These reports include recommendations for improvement.

Running parallel to the audit, students in Lisa's class learned about the impact of trash on the environment. This included learning about plastics, ocean pollution, consumer habits, a natural resource consumption comparison between the United States and other countries, and the idea of a carbon footprint. Students also familiarized themselves with the debate taking place in city hall: whether or not to ban plastic bags. They read articles, listened to arguments from both sides, and researched problems caused by trash pollution.

In the end, students wrote persuasive letters supported by evidence and sent them to both the mayor and their state lawmakers. A couple of the state representatives wrote back, thanking students for their work and letters. Soon thereafter, the city council voted 5–0 to ban plastic bags.[16]

Even if the letters were not the deciding factors in the final vote, the students could still feel as though they participated in the conversation. They learned what it means to be informed citizens and how decisions are made on a local level. Laws like the plastic bag ban affect the daily lives of students and their families, and it is important for them to see that there is a public process behind them, a process to which they can contribute.

A NOTE ABOUT URBAN ENVIRONMENTAL EDUCATION

Because of our school's urban location, all of the examples in this chapter take place in the city. Traditionally, environmental science, or "nature studies," is thought of as taking place in rural areas, or at least in places less developed by humans. City schools may have outdoor classrooms or nearby parks, but a visit to a forest or other ecosystems might mean a long and cost-prohibitive bus ride or an overnight trip. Some states or districts have addressed this challenge by creating "outdoor schools," weeklong residential programs where students learn about ecology while sleeping in rustic cabins.

The place-based approach offers another option for urban schools. According to this model, "environmental" education does not just mean the study of nature separate from human development. It is the study of the environment in which we live: human-made, natural, and the overlap of the two. This gives us the opportunity to apply environmental education to our school, neighborhood, or city without having to leave the metropolitan area.

In fact, there is an emerging field of teaching called urban environmental education (UEE) that focuses on the study of nature in the city. Several environmental education graduate programs now offer courses in UEE, preparing educators for a future where the vast majority of Americans will live in a metropolitan area.[17]

Antioch University and IslandWood in Seattle have created a UEE master's program that goes a step further by extending its focus to social justice, urban planning, and socioecological well-being. According to the program's website,

> The UEE program integrates learning about urban ecology and the built infrastructure with a deep understanding of the social dynamic that determines equity, access and just decision-making. Not all people have access to green spaces and many are as concerned about access to shelter and food, clean air and water and safety as a first priority. Urban environmental educators are challenged to create new place-based experiential approaches that use the city as a classroom incorporating these real issues into outdoor and environmental learning.[18]

This forward-thinking program recognizes the importance of integrating environmental studies and civics by acknowledging that social and environmental justice are closely interconnected. As with place-based education, UEE acknowledges that one of our primary goals as educators is to empower citizens to make positive change in their communities.[19]

Most elementary environmental education programs probably haven't made the social justice leap yet. As a first step, we can consider it our responsibility to teach children that nature and society do not exist in isolation from one another, and that living sustainably is a necessity in the 21st century.

Dog waste and plastic bags are not topics assigned in science textbooks. However, there are many disciplinary core ideas enmeshed within the units, including topics such as natural resources, human impacts on earth systems, interdependent relationships in ecosystems, and more. The checklist grows when we highlight links to language arts and social studies, not to mention math, engineering, and technology.

Like many subject areas, science includes both content and skills that students need to learn. The Next Generation Science Standards emphasize skills more than some past science curriculum frameworks. Approaching science through urban environmentalism, citizen science, and place-based projects naturally addresses many standards while also giving students valuable experience with STEM-based career skills. Students are not just learning content in a vacuum; they see real-world application. This makes place-based education both a viable and a valuable way to address science education in our schools at every grade level.

RESOURCES

The Guide to Education for Sustainability, published by Shelburne Farms' Sustainable Schools Project (2015), offers tools for curriculum design and several project examples.

Scientific American's Citizen Science page offers links to dozens of local and national science projects looking for volunteer researchers. https://www.scientificamerican.com/citizen-science/

Questing: A Guide to Creating Community Treasure Hunts by Delia Clark and Steven Glazer (2006) is a complete guide to creating quests. It even offers a step-by-step procedure for planning a unit, including specific lessons and suggestions for small-group topics.

A People's Curriculum for the Earth: Teaching Climate Change and the Environmental Crisis, edited by Bill Bigelow and Tim Swinehart (2014), clearly connects science education, sustainability, and social justice through articles, simulations, poems, and role plays.

Hungry Coyote, written by Cheryl Blackford and illustrated by Laurie Caple (2015), is a great story to introduce the topic of wild animals living in urban environments.

The Works: Anatomy of a City by Kate Ascher (2005) uses New York City as a model for exploring urban infrastructure features, such as water, traffic, sewage, and electricity.

NOTES

1. Orr, David. 1992. *Ecological Literacy: Education and the Transition to a Postmodern World*. Albany, NY: SUNY Press.

2. Cirillo, Jennifer, and Emily Hoyler. 2015. *The Guide to Education for Sustainability*. Shelburne, VT: Shelburne Farms' Sustainable Schools Project. Accessed May 11, 2017. http://sustainableschoolsproject.org/sites/default/files/EFSGuide2015b.pdf.

3. Hathaway, Susan. Personal communication with author, April 25, 2017.

4. Floum, Jessica. 2017. "Portland Finds Parasite in Drinking Water, Raising Possible Need for Treatment Plant." *Oregonian*, February 6. Accessed May 11, 2017. http://www.oregonlive.com/environment/index.ssf/2017/02/portland_finds_parasite_in_dri.html.

5. Schmidt, Brad. 2016. "Portland Must Reduce Lead in Water Now, State Says." *Oregonian*, November, 9. Accessed May 11, 2017. http://www.oregonlive.com/portland/index.ssf/2016/11/portland_must_reduce_lead_in_w.html.

6. Schmidt, Brad. 2012. "Anti-Fluoride Group Will Submit More Than 35,000 Signatures to Portland in 'Confident' Bid to Force Vote." *Oregonian*, October 10. Accessed May 11, 2017. http://www.oregonlive.com/portland/index.ssf/2012/10/anti-fluoride_group_will_submi.html.

7. Rayman, Noah. 2014. "Portland Dumps 28 Million Gallons of Water after Man Pees into Reservoir." *Time*, April 17. Accessed May 11, 2017. http://time.com/66459/portland-reservoir-pee.

8. Kight, Caitlin. 2012. "A Brief History of Citizen Science." *Science 2.0*, August 24. Accessed May 12, 2017. http://www.science20.com/anthrophysis/brief_history_citizen_science-93317.

9. Feyerabend, Paul. 1982. *Science in a Free Society*. London: New Left Books.

10. Project Feederwatch. "Project Overview." Accessed May 12, 2017. http://feederwatch.org/about/project-overview.

11. National Research Council of the National Academies. 2012. "Dimension 1: Scientific and Engineering Practices," in *A Framework for K-12 Science Education: Practices, Crosscutting Concepts, and Core Ideas*. Washington, DC: National Academic Press.

12. Next Generation Science Standards Lead States. 2013. "MS-ESS2-1 Earth's Systems." Accessed May 12, 2017. http://www.nextgenscience.org/pe/ms-ess2-1-earths-systems.

13. Ibid.

14. City of Portland. 2017. "3d. Urban Forest," in *Portland Plan Atlas*. Accessed May 12. http://www.portlandonline.com/portlandplan/index.cfm?a=288088&c=52254.

15. NGSS Lead States, "MS-ESS2-1 Earth's Systems."

16. Slovic, Beth. 2011. "Portland Approves Ban on Plastic Bags That Takes Effect Oct. 15." *Oregonian*, July 21. Accessed May 11, 2017. http://www.oregonlive.com/portland/index.ssf/2011/07/portland_adopts_ban_on_plastic.html.

17. Westcott, Lucy. 2014. "More Americans Moving to Cities, Reversing the Suburban Exodus." *The Atlantic*, March 27. Accessed May 11, 2017. https://www.theatlantic.com/national/archive/2014/03/more-americans-moving-to-cities-reversing-the-suburban-exodus/359714. Lambert, Lisa. 2012. "More Americans Move to Cities in Past Decade—Census." Reuters, March 26. Accessed May 11, 2017. http://www.reuters.com/article/usa-cities-population-idUSL2E8EQ5AJ20120326.

18. IslandWood. 2017. "Philosophy." Accessed May 11, 2017. https://islandwood.org/graduate-programs/seattle/philosophy.

19. Thomashow, Cynthia, IslandWood UEE graduate program codirector. E-mail message to author, October 10, 2016.

CHAPTER 4

Making History Local and Relevant

A River Ran Wild by Lynn Cherry is a wonderful children's book about the history of the Nashua River in New Hampshire. Each full-page illustration reveals the river at a different time in history: prehistoric, pre-Columbian, the first white settlers, the first towns and mills, industrial, and postindustrial. It is fascinating to see one place change so much over time, and it is fun for children to think how a book about *their* town or city could unfold.

What makes a place unique? Climate and biome play prominent roles in distinguishing regions across continents. But some of the most significant factors are derived from the man-made landscape and the stories that come with it.

Sometimes it is easy to overlook these differences in America, where we often find a lot of "sameness." Commonalities across state lines, such as big box stores and fast food restaurants, can lull our kids into thinking that all places in our country are essentially the same. A standardized, human-made landscape covers up the rich variation in our regional histories and cultures. It can contribute to a disconnection from our place.

Rethinking how we teach history is one way we can reconnect young people with the towns and cities where they live. When they become more familiar with the past, they are better able to understand the complex dynamics at work in their communities and effectively plan for the future.

APPLYING PLACE-BASED THEORY TO HISTORY UNITS

The theory of place-based education suggests that the more we know about where we live and its history, the more we will care about it. This practice can also influence our feelings and actions toward other places and people. By applying the place-based lens, we are fine-tuning historical studies for relevance and usefulness.

Make History Relevant: Connect the Big Story to Local and Personal Experiences

"Why do we need to know this?" students often ask when learning history. "What does this have to do with me?" It is our job to justify the study of history by connecting it as authentically as possible to our students' lives and the places where they live. This is easier to do with more "recent" history.

For example, almost every part of the country was affected by the Great Depression and World War II. It is just a matter of finding the connections that may still be visible in physical features in our towns and cities such as statues and public art. Residents who experienced the history firsthand can serve as living testaments to these events: soldiers, pilots, nurses, widows, children. We can give our students hands-on experience as historians while coming face-to-face with powerful stories that will stay with them forever.

Connecting student experience to ancient history can be more difficult, but it can still be done by looking at big ideas and themes. Studying Hammurabi's Code is a great way to spark a conversation with students about why we have laws and rules today. It is also fun to look at the consequences for breaking rules in Hammurabi's time and compare them to the penalties of today. Talk about a great segue into a discussion of the Eighth Amendment's protection against cruel and unusual punishment!

An examination of ancient Greek democracy and the Roman Empire can serve as crucial background material for a study of our own time and government, through comparison and contrast. Ancient world history does not play a significant role in place-based education in America, but if applied thoughtfully, it can add enrichment to a larger thematic unit.

Historical studies are also made relevant by offering students the opportunity to evaluate their own beliefs and values. When studying the Civil Rights Movement, we can ask our students, "What would you do?" and "How do *you* define courage?" When studying WWII and the Holocaust, we can look more closely at racial and ethnic slurs that are still used in our schools today and learn how they fit into a continuum of discrimination and dehumanization. These examples make history relevant because they directly connect our students with the human experience across time.

Make History Useful: Big Skills-Based Units

Central to any historical unit of study should be this essential question: *What does it mean to be a historian?* Students practice many skills that real historians use, such as observing and inferring, identifying primary and secondary sources, conducting research and interviews, and working to solve mysteries. Invariably, these units go deep into one period in history or one historical theme. The focus is depth rather than scope. However, once students learn the skills of a historian, including critical thinking, they will be able to apply this knowledge to any content they choose. Our role as teachers is not to relay the entirety of world history, but to relate the exciting and engaging process of historical investigation.

History Offers Insights into How to Build the World We Want

As citizens of an ever-evolving democracy, we already have a lens through which we must examine the past: we need to learn how other societies and governments functioned and the role the average citizen played. What was the relationship between the governed and those in power? How did these dynamics lead to events such as war, rebellion, or collapse? What are the real threats to a democracy? Or is there wisdom we could glean and apply to our own situation? Continuously and critically comparing our society and government to others makes history both useful and relevant.

Exploring historical events from multiple perspectives, especially the viewpoints of underrepresented groups, can better teach the whole story and reveal to students the complex dynamics of different cultures living, working, and struggling with and against one another. From this we can extract lessons on what was successful and what wasn't, and better articulate a future that works for everyone.

OUTLINE OF A PLACE-BASED HISTORY UNIT: CIVIL RIGHTS AND PORTLAND'S BLACK HISTORY

The Civil Rights Movement is an ideal entry point into the study of place-based history. This era offers many important lessons for our students. At the Cottonwood School, we decided that the movement was going to be part of our history curriculum because we wanted to impart its message of courage, compassion, and perseverance to our students. By studying the movement, we can learn more about our own potential for bravery. History is made by the heroism of thousands of everyday people, not just a famous few.

But this decision posed some logistical problems for us. First, how would we create local connections in Portland to historical events that primarily took place in the South? A closer examination of this question brought us to a second conundrum. Portland has recently been tagged the "whitest city in America."[1] If this statistic is true, then how did it become that way? What events or actions took place to create this present-day reality? What part did civil rights and the movement play? We soon discovered that this history unit would be a key to helping us and our students better understand our city, its demographics, and our place in this narrative.

Becoming a Historian

When you delve deep into local history, you are also choosing to become an active historian. Although some cities' agencies and local historical societies design curricular resources for teachers, most often you will need to start from scratch. This can certainly be more time-consuming than purchasing a premade resource, but it also can be exciting.

As you uncover the hidden stories of your town or city, it is easy to feel like a detective. This sense of enthusiasm and discovery can be contagious to your students. You become an expert, and besides, the nitty-gritty work needs to be done only one time. Once you have a good unit, you can reuse it, adding any newly uncovered information or sources as you go.

To design the civil rights curriculum at the Cottonwood School, we had to first educate ourselves about local African American history. Our research took us first to the Oregon Historical Society and the library. We were somewhat surprised to find that not many resources on the topic existed, gleaning information from an array of newspaper articles and other primary source documents. We next interviewed Darrell Millner, the head of the black studies department at Portland State University. Through this conversation, we were able to construct a narrative of Portland's black history. Dr. Millner also provided us with primary and secondary sources, including a short documentary from Oregon Public Broadcasting.

Portland's civil rights history, as we learned, is both fascinating and terrible. Oregon's original constitution banned African Americans from living in the state. Even as late as the 1950s, many towns and cities had "sundown" laws that prohibited African Americans from being within the town boundaries after dark. Jim Crow laws in Oregon were considered the most severe this side of the Mississippi. Portland did not prohibit segregation in stores and hotels until years after other West Coast states outlawed the practice, and even then the state had to override a local vote against integration.

One of the most dramatic tales is of the Vanport flood in the 1940s that demolished a low-lying part of the city, originally built for ship workers. City officials knew that the dikes holding back the Columbia River were going to give way, but they did not evacuate the area because they couldn't find another neighborhood (besides Albina, the one neighborhood that was already designated by realtors as the only place black residents could reside) that would agree to house this group of racially integrated refugees. Some historians have compared this incident to the more devastating (but similar) flood in New Orleans caused by Hurricane Katrina.

Redlining practices by Portland banks and realtors resulted in a highly segregated city, which led to segregated schools. This dynamic, along with the continual displacement of the African American community in Portland and on-going problems with police brutality, are still significant problems in our city.[2]

Through research we also discovered the brave individuals of Portland's African American community who fought to change laws and set up support organizations: doctors, community organizers, ministers, lawyers, writers, and educators. Many of the notable activists are still alive or have family members living in the city.

Teaching the Skills: Using Primary Sources

We identified eight essential topics and events for understanding Portland's civil rights history, starting with the Exclusionary Laws of the mid-1800s and ending with the ongoing issue of segregation in our schools. For each topic, we selected a collection of primary sources including photos, newspaper articles, maps, deeds, and other documents.

Students split into eight groups, each of them with a different set of source materials. Their task was to log observations and inferences about what they saw and read. Each group shared the story they pieced together based on the documents. In this way, students used the skills of real historians by working with primary sources and making informed guesses. They went through the discovery process, just as their teachers had when they researched the history.

The activity was challenging because students were not spoon-fed the conclusions and they had to think critically. At the same time, because the documents had been preselected, the activity was not so challenging that it would result in information overload or frustration, which can lead to mental shutdown. We want these forays into historical detective work to pique students' interest and show that they can be successful.

Once students presented their theories about the different historical events, they read short secondary sources that outlined the real story. Groups were able to see where they guessed correctly and fill in missing gaps of information. At this point, groups were now prepared to teach the rest of the class about their part of the narrative.

Making It Real: Fieldwork

If we operate on the idea that the city is our classroom, then it makes sense to get our students out into the field as much as possible. In the civil rights unit, we wanted the students to actually see and stand in the places where history had taken place.

We identified seven locations across Portland for small groups to visit with parent chaperones. We provide the groups with a map of the city, indicating each location, and a clue telling them where to go first. At each stop, students read about the site and answered a couple of short journal questions. The questions were site-specific; they asked students to look for clues, sketch details, or talk to people. Each group also had a camera to take photos of the location. As a finishing touch, we included a list of quotes from civil rights leaders and some sidewalk chalk and encouraged students to write a quote before they departed for the next stop (photo 4.1).

During the course of the afternoon, students saw where the city of Vanport once stood before it was wiped out by floodwaters. The site is now a large city park and golf course. Students visited a park where a riot had broken out in the turbulent days of the late 1960s, located

Photo 4.1. Writing quotes from civil rights leaders while on the Portland Black History scavenger hunt.
Photo by Jim Cartwright

in the middle of a neighborhood where mostly African American residents lived until a recent wave of gentrification pushed them out. They stopped by Vancouver Avenue First Baptist Church, where some of the largest civil rights rallies were held and where Martin Luther King Jr. actually visited. Students also investigated Memorial Coliseum, which had been built after hundreds of African American families were displaced in the 1950s.

Students and their parents were surprised to learn that African Americans have undergone such hardships in Portland. History, and the meaning behind it, came to life. One student, a 7th grade girl who was not always easily "recruitable," exclaimed, "That was the best field trip I've ever been on!"

Making the Human Connection

In the days following the site visits, we continued our study of civil rights in Portland. We interviewed seniors at a community center run by the Urban League and heard firsthand about neighborhood segregation and discrimination. We visited the main offices of the Urban League, which had recently published a study documenting the current status of Portland's African American population in terms of health, education, employment, and other areas. The minister from Vancouver Avenue First Baptist Church came in to speak to the class, sharing his personal story and the current work of his church community.

We watched the documentary produced by Oregon Public Broadcasting. When students wrote biographies of famous civil rights activists, some were assigned local people. One student was able to interview the grandchildren of Portland's first black doctor, Dr. DeNorval Unthank, and another student conducted a phone interview with Ron Herndon, the chairman of the board for the National Head Start Association, a major voice for the desegregation of Portland schools.

We found that the struggle for civil rights is far from over. Segregation and discrimination are not mistakes of the past that were solved by the movement. But the average citizens who put their lives on the line to fight for equality and justice left a legacy. Change does not always come from the most powerful and the most privileged; it can be determined by the people and attained through peaceful means. The important lessons we learned from activists—both national and local, past and present—were ones that we could implement in our own lives, in our own city.

Celebration: Finding an Authentic Audience

Learning the history of African Americans in Portland was incredibly empowering for our students. They felt as if they knew more about the topic than most adults living in the city—and rightly so. The last and crucial piece in this process was sharing the knowledge. It was now their responsibility to become teachers and perhaps even activists.

As a culminating event, we worked with a local playwright/director to create vignettes based on each of the local topics. Each small group of students specialized in one topic, crafting a short script that illustrated the central conflict, using specific historical references. The director linked the stories together with music from the Civil Rights Movement and audio from Martin Luther King Jr.'s "I Have a Dream" speech. We put together a program that gave more historical background for each vignette and performed the piece in a theater downtown to a packed audience.

Most of the people who came to see it were parents and extended family members, but several members of Vancouver Avenue First Baptist Church also attended, including the minister. When the skit about their church started, they clapped and cheered. This was one of the highlights. We made real connections with a community group whom we never would have met if we hadn't reached out.

The second time we taught this unit, the class partnered with a nonprofit that publishes comic books about local history. We hired an artist-in-residence and the class created a comic book telling the story of African Americans in Portland. We printed enough to share with the immediate community and also made it available online. Students presented the comic book to parents and other interested parties in a ceremony hosted by the Oregon Historical Society.

More Connections: The Big Story and Other Disciplines

As we completed this local study we continued to learn about the Civil Rights Movement in the South, linking it to events in Portland.

To learn about the national story, we watched excerpts from the extraordinary documentary *Eyes on the Prize* and read secondary sources published by Teaching Tolerance.

Students also read novels set during the civil rights struggle and participated in literature circles. When writing biographies, students refined their research, writing, revising, and presentation skills. In the end, the combined national and local study made for a unit that heavily integrated language arts, social studies, performance, and visual arts, creating connections to character traits such as courage, responsibility, service, and empathy.

TEACHING THE MORE DISTANT PAST: THE CIVIL WAR

We make history more personal and relevant when we focus on the human story in any event or era. Connecting to the place where students live makes the story all the more personal. This allows us to compare our experiences with others and gives us the opportunity to instruct our students in positive, powerful civic engagement.

This approach can especially impact how we teach about war. History textbooks tend to concentrate on battles, generals, turning points, and so on. But if we focus primarily on the military and strategic aspect of conflict, we lose the human story. We are looking at history through the eyes of the few in power, not the multitudes who lived through the experience of fighting, dying, or just struggling day to day. We also miss the opportunity to hear from those who opposed wars or who had other ideas for resolving conflicts. It is essential that we show our students that there are multiple ways to view conflict as well as alternatives to military action.

Teaching a place-based Civil War unit in Portland, Oregon, posed a similar challenge to teaching about the Civil Rights Movement. The war did not take place here—Oregon had just barely become a state.

Yet, even from a distance, the war had a significant impact on the region. The argument over slavery informed our original constitution (outlawing African Americans), and many soldiers moved here following the war to open businesses and start families. Artifacts from the war are still visible: there are streets named after Civil War generals

(Burnside, Grant, Sherman), statues of soldiers, and cannons from Fort Sumter in a downtown park. We also have cemeteries containing hundreds of Civil War veterans—individual men and women who personally experienced the war before settling in Portland. This is where we decided to base our study.

The national story of the Civil War paralleled our unit. We began with an overview of slavery and the heated debate taking place in the United States around abolition. Students learned about John Brown, Abraham Lincoln, prominent generals, the Emancipation Proclamation, Gettysburg, and Andersonville. At the same time, students started exploring census records from Portland in the 1860s. They learned that most of the people living here at the time were white males. They also learned about common occupations, whether or not most citizens could read, and the typical size of families.

Based on what we knew of America at the time, students made educated guesses about the factors that contributed to these demographics. Students also searched an online database of local newspapers from the time to get a feel for social and political life, being on the lookout for references to the war.

Next, we visited cemeteries. The 8th graders went to the Grand Army of the Republic (GAR) Cemetery (a small and hidden site tucked into the Southwest hills) to look for Union soldiers, and the 7th graders visited Lone Fir Cemetery (a large pioneer burial ground in the middle of SE Portland) to look for Confederate soldiers. The teachers had pre-researched soldiers in the cemeteries and selected ones for whom information was available. Invariably, these were the veterans who had the most interesting stories. Once at the cemetery, students worked in pairs to locate the headstone of their assigned veteran. Using a worksheet, they collected information from the stone and also made a sketch.

Back in the classroom, students searched for primary documents on their veteran using census records, obituaries in contemporary newspapers, and a special census collected in 1890 just for veterans. Some students uncovered many clues through this process; some found very little. But all of them discovered something, even if it was just the veteran's regiment. With that information, students could at least learn which battles the veteran fought in.

As a final step in the research process, students found at least two secondary sources to offer more insight into the experience of their veteran. If the veteran was well-known, the student might have been able to find an article about them. If not, the student looked for more information about the veteran's experience. For example, if their veteran was a member of a colored regiment, they could research information about colored regiments in general.

The GAR cemetery especially yielded incredible finds. We discovered that Salmon Brown, son of John Brown, is buried there. Other notable veterans include a man who served in the regiment that captured John Wilkes Booth, a man who was shot four times by spies and left for dead, a sharpshooter who joined the war when he was 14 years old, a military nurse, a Medal of Honor winner, and a soldier who spent months in the infamous Andersonville prison. Even though Oregon was more than a thousand miles from the fighting, these fantastic connections were literally right under our feet!

After talking to other teachers and citizens of Portland, it became clear that not many people know about these particular Civil War stories. So, what to do with all this information? How to share it with others? Again, this is one of the most essential pieces in the process, where the students become teachers and valuable assets to their community.

We decided to create a quest, using the same format as the geology quest described in the previous chapter. Students first wrote a fact-packed paragraph about their veteran and then condensed it into a six-line rhyming stanza. We linked the "storytelling" clues with movement clues, telling participants where to go next. The treasure box at the end contained a set of laminated cards with more information about the veterans. This is where we included the student-written paragraphs and any photos or graphics the students found. The treasure box also included a sign-in book and a student-made stamp.

The 8th graders presented their final quest to representatives from Metro Regional Government, the agency that manages the cemetery, and posted it on Metro's website and the school's website (photo 4.2).

We've since found that visitors to the cemetery have stumbled upon our quest by accident. A few months after posting the treasure box, we came across this note in the sign-in book:

Photo 4.2. Students read about their veteran on the Civil War Cemetery Quest.
Photo courtesy Metro

I just moved from New York (city and metro area) where I grew up and Williamsburg, Virginia, to West Linn, Oregon. We lived in Virginia for about five years and during that time I visited many Civil War battle sites and GAR cemeteries all over the state. My wife and I became Civil War addicts, you might say. In New York, there is very little Civil War memorialization except for the statue of a Union soldier found in most towns. So I went to many, many Civil War sites in Virginia—Petersburg, Williamsburg, Cold Harbor, and Appomattox to name a few. Nothing moved me more than this remarkable 8th grade project. This humanized the soldiers and the war like nothing I have seen.

I intended to spend a few minutes here, I spent most of the afternoon. I came across this project after walking the cemetery and recognized the names in the Cemetery Quest booklet and went around again and looked at the grave sites with deeper knowledge and appreciation for what these men and women did to preserve the union and free the slaves because now I really knew about them as individuals.

Congratulations CSCS class of 2014 8th grade and your teachers. This is a great project and it must have been terrific working on it.

This feedback from an anonymous "quester" proves the power of learning history on both the local and human scale. It will be hard for students to forget the veteran they spent so much time getting to know. The Civil War now has a face, something that will influence how they reflect upon conflicts in their own time.

THE IMPORTANCE OF MISTAKES

When George Santayana wrote, "Those who cannot remember the past are condemned to repeat it," he encouraged us to think of history as a set of lessons—mainly in what to avoid doing again in the future. Although it can be equally important and potentially more empowering to look for examples of success, there is a lot to be said for learning from our mistakes. The story of World War II gives us the opportunity to approach history from both angles.

As a part of their larger study of the Second World War, for example, our 7th and 8th graders took a closer look at Executive Act 9066 and the internment of Japanese Americans in Portland. Students visited the Oregon Nikkei Legacy Center for an introduction to the topic, took a walking tour of the part of downtown Portland that used to be Japantown before the war, and traveled to the Expo Center, where Portland incarcerated local Japanese Americans until they were forcibly relocated to camps farther inland. Students visited our partner retirement community where they heard from four WWII veterans and had an opportunity to ask questions. A Holocaust survivor also visited the classroom to share her story.

To complete the service-learning cycle, students crafted a scale model of Portland's internment camp for the Nikkei Center's museum (photo 4.3). Students also read Jamie Ford's novel *Hotel on the Corner of Bitter*

Photo 4.3.   Presenting a 3-D map of the Assembly Center, where Japanese American residents of Portland were incarcerated during World War II, to the Nikkei Legacy Center in Portland.
Photo by Chris Wyland

and Sweet about the evacuation of Japanese Americans from Seattle and went on a tour of the locations described in the novel while on their end-of-the-year trip. This unit perfectly illustrates how place-based education makes world history relevant by illuminating a local aspect of a larger story. It also offers valuable insight to our young people at a time when politicians are once again talking about limiting the freedoms of specific religious and cultural groups in the name of national security.

BRINGING HISTORY HOME

Innovative, creative teachers across the country do amazing things to make history more exciting and more engaging. Reenacting events and immersing students in period dress, artifacts, literature, and activities are great ways to tap into students' imaginations and help them to see that people from the past were people just like us but dressed differently. Adding place-based education to the mix brings students one step closer by pushing them beyond the classroom and imagining the past in the places where they live.

Bringing history to life means connecting it to tangible places and ideas. If you are studying the Revolutionary War and you live in the mid-Atlantic, get out and visit sites in your area from that time period. Even if the places were not directly involved in the war, there will still be a connection to the people and issues of the time. Studying the Corps of Discovery is a great entry point into the theme of exploration—no matter where you live. Students can learn and practice navigation skills and maybe even portage a canoe across a football field to get a sense of how hard it was. When we study native peoples, we have the tremendous opportunity to connect with tribes in our area, conduct interviews, and learn about diverse perspectives.

As teachers of history, it is essential that we continuously ask ourselves: What is the "big picture" lesson in this story, the one that transcends time? How can we use it to nurture deeper ties to our communities and encourage stronger, more compassionate leaders for our future? This is how we build curricula that will help ground our students in their place and time while preparing them to be active citizens who value the multiple experiences of people who live there.

RESOURCES

Far Away and Long Ago: Young Historians in the Classroom by Monica Edinger and Stephanie Fins (1998) offers several examples of how to incorporate the skills of a historian into a social studies unit. The project-based ideas examine common historical biases and assume a lens of social justice.

Living Traditions, published by Common Roots in Montpelier, Vermont, is currently out of print and will probably be hard to find, but is one of the best guides out there for designing local history units.

After the Fact: The Art of Historical Detection by James West Davidson and Mark Hamilton Lytle (2009) is a wonderful read for teachers to learn more about how historians "do" history. History is not just a set of facts, but a collection of changing stories dependent on new information. This book introduces the idea of historians as detectives.

Rethinking Columbus: The Next 500 Years, written and edited by Bill Bigelow and Bob Peterson (1998), includes articles and activities to help students sort through the origins of our country by incorporating multiple perspectives, especially Native American. Materials connect past events to current struggles.

A People's History of the United States by Howard Zinn (2005) is the classic alternative text focusing on a working-class, multicultural history. Available in a young adult reader as well, this book is important for teachers to use as a secondary source when planning their American history units, or at least to inform their own understanding.

Free at Last: A History of the Civil Rights Movement and Those Who Died in the Struggle by Sara Bullard (2005) contains a 28-page overview of the Civil Rights Movement, broken into chapters. The overview is followed by 40 profiles of people who died during the struggle, showing students how the movement reached beyond well-known leaders such as Martin Luther King Jr.

America's Civil Rights Movement: A Teacher's Guide by Jeff Sapp (2002) contains 10 ready-to-use activities to accompany the *Free at Last* text.

Hidden History of Civil War Oregon by Randol B. Fletcher (2011) is a great resource for anyone teaching about the Civil War in Oregon. It was a crucial secondary source for Cottonwood School educators while planning the quest.

The Civil War Veteran research packet referenced in this chapter was adapted from a unit created by Jen Kramer.

NOTES

1. Badger, Emily. 2015. "How the Whitest City in America Appears through the Eyes of Its Black Residents." *Washington Post*, March 24. Accessed May 14, 2017. https://www.washingtonpost.com/news/wonk/wp/2015/03/24/how-the-whitest-city-in-america-appears-through-the-eyes-of-its-black-residents/

2. Sherwood, Courtney. 2015. "Protests Disrupt Portland School Board Meeting on Racial Segregation." Reuters, *HuffPost*, January 13. Updated March 15, 2015. Accessed May 14, 2017. http://www.huffingtonpost.com/2015/01/14/portland-school-segregation-protest_n_6467586.html.

CHAPTER 5

Authentic Integration: Addressing Core Content through Place-Based Projects

One of our 5th grade students met a teacher from another school who asked him, "What is your favorite subject? Do you like science?"

The boy replied with the question, "What's science?"

This response did not spring from a deficiency of instruction, but from a school system in which science is not disentangled from social studies, civics, art, and literacy. To him, school is an extension of life and the natural learning process, not a series of subjects.

One of the goals of place-based education, which also corresponds with an effort to inspire lifelong learning, is to remove the boundaries that separate different areas of learning. Place-based projects do not fit into just one content category. Creating divisions between the different disciplines prevents students from recognizing how everything is connected. Classroom teachers reap the most success from place-based units when they are able to integrate curricular goals within project work.

When studying the water quality of a local stream, science may seem like the primary subject. But students also need to research and write reports, present to interested agencies, create attractive materials, learn the human history of the area, and work with statistics. Likewise, a study of restaurant management incorporates reading menus, writing receipts, measuring ingredients, speaking to the public, designing interiors, and learning about local agriculture. Highlighting the interconnections is how we make topics relevant and promote lifelong learning.

Place-based units are not "add-ons" that will take away from core content. Curriculum integration provides an effective way to address subject area standards in language arts, science, and math by providing a context for the skills. When students are able to immediately apply what they learn, the understanding is deeper and longer lasting.

As we work to close the achievement gap and keep kids interested in school, it is clear that we need to move toward a more experiential, interdisciplinary model.[1] When students engage in projects that mirror adult undertakings, it is easier for them to feel that school is an exciting part of life—not something set apart. Research suggests that interdisciplinary, project-based learning also helps students retain curricular content and skills better than the traditional approach.[2]

Integrated curriculum could very well be the way of the future. In fact, Finland recently became the first country to shift from a model of traditional school subjects to the interdisciplinary format. The head of Finland's Department of Education explained, "There are schools that are teaching in the old-fashioned way which was of benefit in the beginning of the 1900s—but the needs are not the same, and we need something fit for the 21st century."[3] To keep our students engaged and properly prepare them for lives that will be very different from the experience of someone living during the Industrial Revolution, it may behoove us to follow suit.

The previous two chapters focused on connecting science and history to place-based units. This chapter illustrates how a wide variety of standard-based learning is embedded in projects we have done at the Cottonwood School. As with the history and science projects, these units especially incorporate skills outlined in the Common Core standards. Since skills are not content-dependent, they can be easily applied to any topic.

LANGUAGE ARTS

Reading and writing naturally weave into most place-based units. Nearly all project work requires research in order for students to learn more about a topic. Beyond collecting information firsthand through interviews and surveys, students need to read articles, reports, and primary sources. They will need to write in order to persuade, inform, and convey what they've learned (photo 5.1).

Photo 5.1.   Taking fieldwork notes.
Photo by Sarah Mutal

National standards are increasingly in line with teaching methods used in project- and place-based education. Next Generation Science Standards recognize how science education relies on written communication. Additionally, new Common Core literacy standards stress nonfiction reading and writing, necessary skills for projects in which students are learning about the places where they live.

Globalization and Journalism

Sometimes language arts are at the heart of a project. When our 7th and 8th grade humanities teacher, Emily Conner, launched a unit on global trade and globalization, writing became a primary focus.

Globalization is a fundamental theme of our time. Countries around the world are experiencing political upheaval in response to international trade and migration. The topic hits close to home as both workers and consumers are affected by globalization on a daily basis. At the same time, the profession of journalism—and even the idea of "facts"—is under attack. The globalization project is a great example of how social studies, language arts, and local investigations can combine to help our students make sense of a complicated and timely issue.

Students began the unit by collecting items from home and mapping their origins. They found that Asia, especially China, produces many of the products we buy. But they also found that other countries seem to have specialties. For example, many of the students' bed sheets were produced in Bangladesh.

As an introduction to the unit, students wrote the "invisible story" behind an object from their lives. They chose something of significance to them and used descriptive, narrative, and analytical skills to tell the tale. Students chose everything from items of clothing to musical instruments to a boy's favorite pig pencil case (which became a story about his relationship with his parents—and his desire for a pet pig).

Meanwhile, students completed a mini-unit on the history of trade including topics such as the Silk Road, the Black Plague, and colonialism. During these lessons, students read secondary sources, examined primary sources, took notes, and wrote responses to the texts.

To connect current globalization issues to contemporary literature, Emily read aloud from the book *The Weight of Water* by Sarah Crossan, about a young Polish immigrant in England.

Students also participated in book groups. The public libraries in Portland have a wonderful program called "Bucket of Books," where a classroom teacher can request a variety of books on a particular topic. When Emily asked for young adult novels related to the theme of globalization, the librarians sent her a list of 30. She culled the list to 10, did a book talk for each one, and the students chose the top three they wanted to read. Book groups were designed based on student choice, which invariably included skill level. In addition to discussing the literary virtues of the story, students connected the novels to the overall theme of globalization. (See the Resources section at the end of this chapter for the names of the books.)

The unit incorporated several fieldwork opportunities. Students toured Creo Chocolate in Northeast Portland to learn about the differences between direct trade and fair trade. A local grocery store hosted them for a discussion about local versus global food sourcing. Students traveled to the Nike headquarters just outside of Portland to hear from a trade lawyer and another local trade representative. During this visit they had the opportunity to ask questions and tour the grounds.

Back in the classroom, students demonstrated their learnings through an intensive journalism project. With the help of professional journalist Garrett Andrews, who served as a writer-in-residence, they crafted articles about local products or businesses that have global ties. Garrett explained the role of a journalist (including a conversation about ethics) and led lessons on interviewing, organization, and editing.

Students conducted an interview with someone associated with the product or company they were researching. A couple of girls interviewed a local record shop owner to learn more about a collection of mixtapes featuring international artists that he curated. Another pair of students looked into a Portland jewelry shop that uses sustainable lab-made diamonds to give customers an alternative to the "blood diamonds" mined in several African countries (figure 5.1). Two other students took the opportunity to meet their favorite local writer and artist and learn about translation and the international elements of publishing.

Students then created podcasts based on their articles. To learn more about podcasting, students visited Oregon Public Broadcasting's headquarters and heard from experts in the news studio. Mikey Neilson, creator of the podcast *Chronicles of the Nerds*, also visited the class to offer examples and tips.

As a culmination, the Oregon chapter of the Society of Professional Journalists shared selected articles. Students also shared the articles and podcasts with the community during a class celebration.

There are over a dozen Common Core literacy standards connected to this unit. Skills include gathering relevant information from multiple sources, conducting a short research project, using technology to produce and publish writing, and writing informative texts to examine a topic and convey ideas. The list grows when you consider the embedded social studies and career skills. There are so many to choose from, it ultimately comes down to which ones the teacher decides to stress and assess. With such a place-based, integrated project, however, the learning clearly goes beyond standards.

Figure 5.1.   Representation of locally made diamonds as part of globalization unit.
Drawing by Zoey Ford and Dayva Cockrell

Quests as a Venue for Literacy Skills

The previous two chapters contained examples of quests. Quests are a fun and useful way to organize a place-based unit, and their flexible format makes them applicable to a diversity of topics. Whatever content you explore with a quest, you will need to teach literacy skills. Students read informational and historical texts to glean essential details. They also convey facts through clear, expository paragraphs.

When the 4th and 5th graders created the geology quest for downtown Portland, they designed informational cards for the treasure box. These cards gave information about each location, including details about rock type and building history. Here is one student's example:

At the Unitus Plaza, travertine is everywhere! Travertine is a sedimentary rock. It contains calcium carbonate and is usually found polished. Travertine is formed when hot springs evaporate, and the minerals from the water clump together. The clumps go into caves and catch more sediments. Over time, these sediments build up and form rock. The largest building to be made of travertine is the Colosseum in Rome. Travertine is a very decorative rock. It is sometimes mistaken for marble, except marble is metamorphic and travertine is sedimentary. Travertine is formed near hot springs, and is used for many things like tables, chairs, and bathroom floor tiles, too.

Similarly, for the 8th grade Civil War Veteran quest at the Portland Grand Army of the Republic Cemetery, two boys wrote the following informational paragraphs about the veteran John Millington:

John W. Millington was an American hero who assisted in the capture of John Wilkes Booth, the infamous assassin of Abraham Lincoln. Millington joined the army in 1861 in the 93rd Infantry of New York. He received an unfortunate case of typhoid and left for a year to get better. A year later he joined the 16th NY Cavalry. In 1865, he participated in the hunt for John Wilkes Booth.

Millington and his regiment hunted for Booth for two days in Virginia. Eventually, Booth was found at a farm where he and his accomplices were hiding in a barn. The cavalry surrounded the barn and asked them to come out. Booth and his men said no. David Herold, one of the accomplices, surrendered and was tied to a tree. Millington was told to guard him. Despite Herold saying that he didn't know that Booth would kill Lincoln, he was hanged. In the end, Millington ended up living in Oregon for 26 years. This is the story of John W. Millington.

Quests traditionally employ rhyming couplets to provide clues to the reader. Teaching how to write rhyming couplets becomes part of the curricular content, whether the quest is based in history, civics, art, or science. Here is the stanza the boys wrote about Millington:

I was in the 16th New York Cavalry in the war,
For a while, typhoid took me out of the tour.
I helped to capture John Wilkes Booth.
We set fire to the old barn roof.

Abraham Lincoln was my superior.
To him, I felt quite inferior.
In the battle of Gettysburg I fought,
Luckily I survived and was never caught.

Teaching students how to write couplets could easily connect to a poetry unit where students learn about other rhyme schemes and famous poets.

As a literacy extension, students can also write historical fiction. Primary sources such as census records, obituaries, and gravestones, along with secondary sources on the time period, can help students construct stories about the veterans (in the case of John Millington, an action story!) while interweaving historical fact. These stories can be published with historical societies, compiled into a book, or adapted into a play.

As is the case with most place-based projects, quests offer students an authentic audience. This makes all the difference in terms of student investment and also heightens effort and performance. Additionally, students create developmentally appropriate reading and research material about local people and places for future students, something that is often difficult for primary teachers to find.

The Importance of Writing for an Audience Outside of the School

By Kate McPherson

One way to pump up student engagement is for students to publish their work for authentic audiences. Kate McPherson, who has served as school improvement and service-learning consultant for many years, recently worked at Roosevelt High School in Portland, helping to establish a writing and publishing center. Unique Ink, the student-led publishing center, works alongside classroom teachers to help students have a valued audience beyond the classroom.

For the last few years, freshman language arts teachers have taught students how to write informative essays through our Freedom

Fighter Project. After investigating the importance of social justice and the impact of marginalization, students choose an issue that interests them and they interview someone who has done extraordinary work in our community. As students work on their essays, they care more about the quality of their work because they want the story in our traveling museum exhibit and book to accurately convey the spirit of the person as well as their work. They want to represent *their* freedom fighter well. Students then take the exhibit and their writing into the community—to city hall, county commissioner chambers, and churches, and a reception is held at the Oregon Historical Society. Students have an increased sense of pride when the community members come up, ask them about the people being interviewed, and genuinely value their work.

The mock trial class partnered with our publishing center to create a book that helps youth and parents understand their rights and stay safe when interacting with police. One of our students was tased by the police, and it was determined that this was an overuse of power on the part of the police. Rather than just go on with the regular curriculum, students generated questions they had about their rights and gathered helpful information through research and personal conversations. (They interviewed more than 30 community members.) They have now published a book that addresses the questions youth raised. This summer, youth will work with the local NAACP to refine a comic that depicts common scenarios where youth interact with law enforcement, and they will develop a training and animation and begin providing training throughout the community.

In addition, our creative writing teacher teamed with the 3rd grade teacher in our feeder elementary school to create children's books that reflect the lives and places our children experience. These books have been purchased by the school district to be part of the district's early literacy initiative.

Research by Fred Newmann identifies qualities that are present in learning experiences that more effectively engage secondary students. One of those central qualities is having an authentic audience beyond the classroom. Our publishing center helps provide the support teachers need to forge community connections that provide a deeper purpose for classroom learning.

VISUAL ARTS

Art is often part of place-based projects. For example, a nature guide for a local park may require botanical drawings and a hand-drawn map. Students have good reason to practice and improve artistic skills when they make a product for an authentic audience.

Planning projects in conjunction with art teachers can make for a rich, integrated experience that is mutually beneficial. From the art teacher's perspective, the skills learned are immediately applied. From the classroom perspective, the supportive instruction helps to increase the product quality.

Including an art element in a project can also be a hook for students. Some kids feel passionate about writing and reading, some shine when interviewing and presenting, and others excel in the visual arts. Providing multiple ways for students to access a project allows for more success and engagement over a range of abilities and interests.

Medicinal Plant Art Installation

A few years ago, Portland's National University of Natural Medicine (NUNM) asked if we would like two garden beds located on their campus. The university had created a public garden for children in order to build partnerships with local schools. Even though the campus is a bit of a walk from our school, we of course said yes.

That same fall we were introduced the work of local artist Nina Montenegro. Nina's art can be considered place-based. According to her website (NinaMontenegro.com), her practice "crosses disciplines to advocate for an ecologically-viable and socially-just future." Nina had recently painted a mural in North Portland called *Plants Around Us*, depicting several of the edible and medicinal plants growing in the immediate area.

We thought that our new partnership with NUNM would be a wonderful way for us to connect art and botany. After talking with both Nina and the university, we discovered that all parties were equally excited. We applied for and received a grant from the Regional Arts and Culture Commission in Portland to hire Nina as an artist-in-residence to work with our 5th and 6th graders during the spring trimester.

Nina proposed creating an art installation similar to the one she created in North Portland for the school garden space on the NUNM campus. In exchange, the university faculty and students volunteered to teach our kids about the properties of medicinal plants. Once the students learned the plant basics, Nina led lessons on botanical drawing. Students made sketches in the field and then created final drafts in the classroom. Then over a series of sessions, they transferred their drawings onto large wooden panels and painted them.

Meanwhile, teachers Lisa Columbo and Karinsa Kelly connected the art project to a botany unit in the classroom where students compared plant cells to their own cheek cells, created cell analogies to learn about the functions of organelles, and studied photosynthesis using an online inquiry lab. They also planted the same medicinal plants they had been studying in the garden plots donated by the university.

The final art product consisted of 19 separate panels, each one depicting a different medicinal plant. At the unveiling ceremony students read original poems about the different plants and handed out postcard books featuring art from the installation (photo 5.2).

Clearly, there were many benefits to conducting this project, art education being just one. Looking through the lens of an art educator, however, there were many places where the work connected to standards. Students practiced drafting and revising their drawings, they considered style and color when designing the panels, they worked with a professional artist, and they held a public presentation of their work. Again, giving their art an authentic audience engaged students on a different level than if they were creating for only their teacher. Place-based projects can show students how art is relevant in the "real world."

What Is a Neighborhood?

Our 1st and 2nd graders looked closely at what makes a neighborhood using the city as their learning laboratory. Their culminating project turned out to be another work of art intended for the public.

At the beginning of the unit, the class created a collage on their wall containing houses, streets, shops, and other key locations. Students constructed people out of colorful paper to add to the scene. Each student

Photo 5.2.   Paintings of medicinal herbs on the campus of Portland's National University of Natural Medicine.
Photo by author

chose a character who contributed something important to the neighborhood and spent the trimester journaling and problem-solving from this character's perspective. (Chapter 8 has more details about this process, called Storyline). Even in these early stages of the project the students had many opportunities to engage in artistic activities.

Photo 5.3.   Surveying the neighborhood from the top of a nearby high rise.
Photo by Nesa Levy

Next, teachers Nesa Levy and Megan Richter led students on several forays into the neighborhood surrounding the school to both verify the elements they had proposed in their collage and find new details they may have missed (photo 5.3). The class toured the local bank, explored a nearby hospital, sampled public transit, and visited a fire station. They also invited a community developer into the classroom to talk about future plans for the neighborhood. Students had the chance to ask, "How come we don't have a grocery store here?"

As a culminating project to this unit, students created a coloring book of neighborhood locations to welcome new children to the area. A local business covered printing costs for 1,000 copies and the neighborhood association helped us to distribute books through the farmer's market and other businesses.

Making the book required many steps. After the class had been on several neighborhood walks, they worked to create and refine a list of notable features. Students then signed up in small groups to focus on one. The students wrote descriptive sentences for each place, such as, "The streetcar is an electric train that goes around the city" and "There

The streetcar is an electric train that goes around the
city.

Figure 5.2.   A 2nd-grader's portrait of the Portland Streetcar for the neighborhood coloring book.

are many native plants at Cottonwood Bay." Using their own observations and information from local experts, young students had their first opportunity to use the expository mode for sharing information with the public.

The book's main attraction, of course, was the student drawings. Kids worked together and with their teachers to draft illustrations. As part of the process, the class revisited many of the places to see if they had forgotten any important details in their drawings. Back in the classroom, children revised their work to make it more descriptive and accurate. Ultimately, the drawings were outlined in thick marker so that other children could color between the lines (figure 5.2).

Drawing and painting demand that our students look more closely at the world around them. This practice, especially when combined with a service-learning project, makes art an ideal vehicle for place-based education.

MATH

Just as the shift in literacy toward nonfiction can be described as "real-life writing," the application of numeric skills within place-based projects could be coined "real-life math." Almost more than any other subject in school, students demand to know how their lessons in mathematics will be applied to their future. As they get older and the content becomes increasingly abstract, their questioning increases. To keep the majority of our students tuned in, it is important for us to acknowledge their concerns.

Much of the math used in place-based projects is also the math that most of us apply in everyday life, such as making estimates, measuring dimensions, balancing a budget, and calculating weights. More mathematically complex projects may require students to practice skills used by professionals on a daily basis, such as predicting rates or change over time, displaying and analyzing statistics, or collecting and analyzing data.

Keeping students on track with math standards can make it one of the most difficult subjects to integrate. Some topics are easier to connect to a place-based project than others, but the skills need to be taught regardless. At the Cottonwood School, all grade levels hold math classes every day to teach necessary skills. If the skills can be connected outside of class to a larger project, great! But it doesn't always work out that way. This doesn't keep us from finding ways to highlight mathematical thinking and processes when they happen. Here are some examples of how math is integrated into our place-based projects:

- Urban tree survey: As part of their survey of trees in our neighborhood, 7th and 8th graders needed to calculate the DBH (diameter at breast height) for each tree and estimate its height. They also determined percentages of species and created graphs and charts to display their data.
- Street car models: Middle school students created scale models of Portland Streetcar cars using blueprints from the United Streetcar company. They applied their knowledge of ratio, as well as practiced their skills with measurement and basic geometry.
- Restaurant unit: 1st and 2nd graders gained hands-on practice with money, addition, and subtraction while making menus and receipts as part of their restaurant management unit. They also gained experience with measurement and fractions during their baking class.

- Water quality testing: Middle school students gained experience with ratios when they determined the percentage of dissolved oxygen in a water source and learned to use phrases such as *parts per million* and *milligrams per liter*. Communicating their results was another opportunity for making graphs and charts.
- Mapping: All grade levels apply math on some level through mapping, including measurement, scale, and geometry.

In addition to hands-on application, we can show our students how math is used in the "real world" by inviting experts into the classroom to talk about their work and share examples. Engineers, data analysts, chefs, and business owners are all professionals who can demonstrate the role math plays in their everyday lives. One of our middle schoolers' favorite guest speaker was an architect who visited as the class prepared to create the scale model of the WWII Japanese internment camp mentioned in chapter 4. Even if it isn't part of an ongoing project, planning a weekly or monthly "guest expert" can be a great way to link math to the community.

Applying "real-life" math is going to be much more easily established for elementary school concepts than math at the middle and high school levels. It is great to highlight connections between more abstract math and project-based work, but don't expect to find straightforward applications for every concept.

Anthony Robinson, a former middle school math teacher from the Cottonwood School, emphasizes the importance of relevance. He states that one of the most important things a math teacher can do "is having the knowledge to connect the material back to the world we live in. From my point of view, you can increase buy-in for many resistant students by simply telling them how the material is used or at least being able to explain where it is going."[4]

Although this might seem like common sense to some of us, for others it may mean doing a bit of research and making more connections.

TECHNOLOGY

As a training ground for the future, schools have a responsibility to incorporate technology into instruction. But how? What is the best way and what skills are most important? Place-based schools and classrooms also need to consider how technology best fits their mission to serve and engage with the community.

Technology can best support place-based projects through product creation. Example products include the podcasts created in the globalization unit and the websites made as part of the water system unit. Interactive scavenger hunts, digital maps, movies, music, and online publications are among other possibilities. By extension, students can also use technology to collaborate on these projects and communicate them to a wider audience.

There are limitations to the Internet as a research source. In a place-based school, information gleaned from the Internet can give an important perspective, but it does not tell the whole story. In order for research to truly inform students' lives, they must find a way to relate it to the place they live. Collecting data from the local community in tandem with reliable online sources can make for a rich, balanced project in which the students feel both rooted and connected to the wider world.

Embracing technology can help capture student buy-in and attract partners who are also working to become more "tech savvy." To make sure technology is not replacing place-based methods for collecting information, it is a good idea to take the time needed to develop a philosophy statement so everyone is on the same page about how, when, and where you will incorporate it into your program.

THE INTEGRATED CLASSROOM

A truly interdisciplinary learning classroom looks quite different from a traditional one. Place-based projects do not often fall into a neatly slotted period of the day. Many teachers who practice place-based education have a "project time" that is specially set aside for some of this work. For some teachers, project time is a few times a week; for others it is every day.

There is not just one way for a teacher's schedule to accommodate place-based projects, but it does often require some degree of flexibility. Schools that have rigid schedules and hard demarcations between subject areas make it more difficult for integrated, community-based learning to flourish. It is possible for a lone teacher to accomplish a small, successful place-based project, but this is not the same as a schoolwide effort to immerse students in community-based education and civic engagement.

Teachers who teach one subject, like high school English, can certainly design place-based projects in their classrooms. Most likely these projects will focus on reading and writing, but they will intrinsically draw from other subjects. Collaborating with other teachers is a key strategy in schools where teachers specialize, even if it is simply to integrate students' background knowledge from other classes.

Integrated learning can feel scary, especially when teachers are under pressure to cover a certain amount of content in a year. But when we see all of the ways that different subjects connect and overlap, it becomes increasingly difficult to "unsee" them. Once we recognize the interdisciplinary nature of a topic, place-based projects provide a strategy for addressing a wide range of required standards across multiple subject areas. Situating lessons in meaningful local projects offers a more engaging way for students gain the necessary skills and knowledge we are required to teach.

RESOURCES

The Complete Guide to Service Learning: Proven, Practical Ways to Engage Students in Civic Responsibility, Academic Curriculum, and Social Action by Cathryn Berger Kaye (2010) provides multiple tools for planning integrated service-learning projects. The book includes several example topics complete with project ideas, interdisciplinary connections, and both fiction and nonfiction supporting texts.

Starting from Scratch: One Classroom Builds Its Own Curriculum by Steven Levy (1996) is an inspirational book about a 4th grade teacher's experience designing curriculum for an integrated classroom.

Rethinking Globalization: Teaching for Justice in an Unjust World, edited by Bill Bigelow and Bob Peterson (2002), is the essential resource for any teacher wishing to explore this important topic. It includes articles, poems, activities, and simulations.

Rethinking Mathematics: Teaching Social Justice by the Numbers by Eric Gutstein and Bob Peterson (2013) offers teachers examples of how to integrate math into social studies, language arts, and more through the lens of social justice.

A Place for Wonder: Reading and Writing Nonfiction in the Primary Grades by Georgia Heard and Jennifer McDonough (2009) shows how nonfiction writing can be just as engaging and exciting as fiction. This is an important foundation for a place-based school.

Literacy for Science: Exploring the Intersection of Next Generation Science Standards and Common Core for Literacy Standards (2014) from the National Academies Press can further aid teachers who are leading science-based projects.

More Mirrors in the Classroom: Using Urban Children's Literature to Increase Literacy by Jane Fleming, Susan Catapano, Candace M. Thompson, and Sandy Ruvalcaba Carrillo (2016) is a resource to help teachers integrate literature into urban classrooms that better reflects the experiences of their students.

Novels read in book groups during the globalization unit:

- *Threads* by Ami Polonsky (2016)
- *Now Is the Time for Running* by Michael Williams (2013)
- *The Seventh Most Important Thing* by Shelley Pearsall (2016)
- *Something In Between* by Melissa de la Cruz (2016)
- *Home of the Brave* by Katherine Applegate (2008)
- *Red Glass* by Laura Resau (2009)

Visit NinaMontenegro.com to view more photos of the art installation on the NUNM campus (The "Plants Around Us: Galen's Way" project) and to learn more about Nina's work.

NOTES

1. Bridgeland, John M., John J. Dilulio Jr., and Karen Burke Morison. 2006. *The Silent Epidemic: Perspectives of High School Dropouts.* A report by Civic Enterprises in association with Peter D. Hart Research Associates for the Bill & Melinda Gates Foundation.

2. Edutopia. 2008. "Why Teach with Project-Based Learning?: Providing Students with a Well-Rounded Classroom Experience." Last modified February 28, 2008. Accessed September 6, 2017. https://www.edutopia.org/project-learning-introduction.

3. Global Research. 2016. "Finland Will Become the First Country in the World to Get Rid of All School Subjects." Last Modified February 2, 2017. Accessed September 6, 2017. http://www.globalresearch.ca/finland-will-become-the-first-country-in-the-world-to-get-rid-of-all-school-subjects/5572373.

4. Personal communication with author, January 23, 2017.

CHAPTER 6

The Civic Classroom

"Think globally, act locally" is a popular slogan, urging us to align our daily actions with a grander vision for the planet. It's a grassroots approach, acknowledging the importance of small-scale change and education, one that sees large-scale transformation as an accumulation of localized efforts.

Civic education could easily adopt a similar tagline: "Think of the community, act in the classroom." We have an enormous opportunity when we teach civics. Not only can we educate our students how to be involved, active members of society, we can also coach them how to be respectful, accountable members of their classrooms and schools.

We often think of civics as the study of government. But, by definition, civics is the study of the rights and duties of citizenship. There is a definite distinction between the study of government and the study of citizenship. Teaching both is essential.

This chapter explores how we can prepare students for both future citizenship and responsible citizenship right now as they engage with each other and local partners. Place-based education, at its core, is about creating and sustaining healthy communities, and the first steps take place at home, in the classroom.

ESTABLISH COMMUNITY AS A PRIORITY

Kids need be part of a secure group before they can feel responsible for the wider community. Nurturing healthy relationships is just as important in the school as it is in our boardrooms, city halls, and embassies. Students come to our classrooms in the fall bringing with them a diversity of backgrounds and experiences. It is essential for them to connect with one another, learn about their classmates, and share. Students need to know that human relationships are just as important as the curriculum. **ess.**

Here are some examples of how a school can model community as a priority:

Confirm

- Morning meetings: Starting each day with morning meeting is one way to show students that community is a priority in the classroom. These meetings are a simple ritual dedicated to welcoming students to school, greeting each other, and reviewing the daily schedule. Some classrooms play short games or do activities as a way to start the day on a positive note while also building community. This can also be a time for sharing personal stories and announcements. When we take the time to thoughtfully transition from home to school instead of launching immediately into academics, we communicate that we value our students and where they come from.

Surprising

- Teaching lunch: Lunch can be a terrifying time for kids, especially as they get older and social cliques are reinforced in the cafeteria. In our K–8 school, students eat in their classroom with the teacher, affording us the opportunity to "teach" lunch. Lessons can help students be inclusive, initiate a conversation, and practice basic table manners. Again, this practice conveys to students that the health and safety of the group takes precedence over convenience for the teacher.

Surp.

- All-school meetings and student families: Most schools have some format for gathering together, whether it be a weekly assembly or morning announcements. This time is a valuable opportunity to highlight character traits and celebrate classroom achievements. At the Cottonwood School, we have organized our K–8 student body into "families" made up of one student from every grade level. The families sit together during all-school meetings, where the youngest members are overseen by the eldest. Once a month, families meet in classrooms in lieu of all-school meetings, to complete activities and connect to one another.

- Cross-grade programing: In a K–8 school, there are many possibilities for nurturing relationships between the grade levels. Reading buddies, mentoring, and conflict-resolution programs are all ways that students can practice taking care of others in their community. By instilling service as part of the school culture, we prepare students to help on a larger scale.
- Public recognition of community partners: At the Cottonwood School, we turned our largest and most central bulletin board into a "Community Partners" showcase. Every month, a different classroom posts information and photos to educate other students, teachers, and parents about their neighborhood partner. That same month, the class prepares a skit or presentation to share how they worked together. Throughout their time at the Cottonwood School, students see that building relationships with outside organizations and agencies is a school priority.

When students are surrounded by the culture of community, they will feel a sense of belonging. This will lead them to more readily invest in the stories of others. The skills students learn when they create positive relationships with their peers and their teachers are equally valuable in the field when working with neighbors and other adult citizens.

HONOR DIVERSE PERSPECTIVES

In a democracy, citizens must work together to make decisions, pass policies, and govern communities. Our students have the opportunity to practice this process through civic action projects. Once they dig below the surface of any issue, however, they soon find that varying groups of people have divergent interests and opinions. The same can be said for most classroom communities. Giving students tools to honor diverse perspectives serves both the class and the work they do outside of the classroom.

Civil discourse is an endangered skill both in our popular culture and in our political forums. Without explicit training in how to respectfully and intelligently discuss a topic, our young people can easily follow examples set by the adults they see in cable news, in presidential campaigns, or perhaps in their own homes and neighborhoods.

When students are surrounded by incivility, they are not being shown how to think critically or collaboratively. Danielle Wiese Leek, assistant professor in the School of Communications at Grand Valley State University in Allendale, Michigan, says that this negative modeling is not just dangerous, "it's anti-democratic. . . . It's not about learning to be exposed to a variety of perspectives in order to draw the best conclusion. It teaches young people that if they aren't the loudest, their opinion doesn't matter. Second, it shuts down opportunities for collaboration and innovation."[1]

In contrast, civil discourse "supports, rather than undermines, the societal good," according to Kate Shuster, author of Teaching Tolerance's Civil Discourse in the Classroom guide.[2] Shuster points out that this is not about being overly polite or deferential. Instead it means being able to assert your claims clearly, back them up with reasoning and evidence, and listen respectfully to statements made by others. The ultimate priority is not being right, but finding the solutions that best serve the community.

We need to explicitly teach active listening as part of this process. How do you show someone you're listening? What verbal cues do you give? What do you say? How do you start a response? We can't assume that our students come to our classrooms knowing how to do any of these things.

There are multiple benefits to learning the skill of civil discourse. It help students consider alternative perspectives while also giving them a leg up in other areas of academics where they are often asked to form and defend arguments. Beyond school walls, we are in tremendous need of citizens with more of this training. Our students can even set the example for adults in the community.

When students engage with adults outside of the classroom, they will undoubtedly confront a diversity of perspectives. Even public transit rides through the city can expose students to new or unfamiliar realities. Teachers can turn these situations into opportunities to better understand the lives and experiences of others.

A few years ago, our middle school teachers noticed that their students were struggling to make sense of the homelessness problem in Portland. The kids made assumptions based on misinformation and started using derogatory labels for homeless folks, such as "bum" and "hobo."

The teachers contacted a local advocacy group for the homeless and asked if a speaker could come to the class. As it turned out, the four people who came to speak were either previously or currently homeless. They told their personal stories, all different, explaining how they ended up on the streets. The speakers were both vulnerable and honest with the students and, in turn, the students were a rapt, engaged audience. Without this chance to directly hear from people who had experienced homelessness, it would have been easy for the students to carry their assumptions and stereotypes into adulthood.

Honoring diverse perspectives in our classroom offers an end in itself. When we consider the viewpoints of others, we are made to understand that not everyone in our community feels or thinks the same way as us; they have not had our life experience even though they live in the same place. Grappling with this reality, and even learning to appreciate it, brings us one step closer to building more inclusive, respectful communities both in school and out.

POSITIVE PROBLEM-SOLVING

Democratic classrooms and communities need citizens who are willing to roll up their sleeves and tackle problems head-on. But we can't assume that our students know how to do this without instruction, practice, and support.

Class meetings have been the cornerstone for building democratic classrooms in our school for years. Whereas morning meetings are a time for us to connect and share, class meetings are a forum for us to address and solve problems. (We found the inspiration and structure for class meetings in the book *Positive Discipline in the Classroom: Developing Mutual Respect, Cooperation, and Responsibility in Your Classroom.*[3])

The routine is simple. Once or twice a week, all students in a class gather in a circle. After going around and giving each other acknowledgements (another life skill that needs to be explicitly taught and practiced), the teacher or a student facilitator checks the agenda book to see if anyone signed up to bring a problem to the group. If some-one did, they have a chance to explain the situation. Students then go around the circle and everyone has a chance to offer a positive solution. The teacher or a student scribe writes all of the suggestions down in the logbook. The student with the issue can then choose from the list of solutions and the class checks back in with them during the next meeting to see if it helped.

Some problems can be small: pencils keep disappearing from the classroom or there is a disagreement over saving seats. Other issues are more complicated: people have been using hurtful language, or some-one needs help resolving a conflict between two friends. Either way, it is immensely powerful to step back and allow students to present and solve problems as a group without teachers doing it for them.

This doesn't mean that teachers are not heavily involved in guiding the process. It is extremely important for the teacher to set the appropri-ate tone. This is mostly established in the first few weeks of school as the teacher slowly trains students in all the steps of class meetings. In the beginning, teachers are often required to explain how the process benefits students and redirect anyone who is having a hard time staying positive, respectful, or on task. By midyear, however, many classes can run class meetings without a teacher.

Not every solution works, but that is also true in adult life. Classes continually revisit solutions that aren't working and try to find a way to adjust and improve. For a student, the opportunity to speak about a conflict to the community—to be heard—can even be enough to defuse an argument. Students are incredibly empowered by the opportunity to present and solve their own problems without judgement or punish-ment. When the adults in a classroom can trust the young people to self-regulate, the students often rise to the challenge.

Class meetings can be employed at all grade levels, from kindergar-ten to high school. We begin training our 5-year-olds in the process and by the time they are 12 or 13, they are pros. Working together respect-fully as a large group is not an easy task, but it is incredibly valuable work. Place-based projects often call on students to construct and sug-gest solutions to community issues. Giving students the opportunity to practice positive problem-solving on a regular basis in class is perfect preparation for both place-based projects and future citizenship.

Addressing Disrespectful Language with
Positive Problem-Solving

It was the middle of the school year and my class was getting cranky. They had less patience with each other, were snapping at each other more, and their word choice was not always kind.

At a class meeting, a couple of students brought up the issue of disrespectful language. Everyone agreed that it was happening, and because we approached the topic in a nonpunitive, nonjudgmental way, everyone admitted that they were sometimes at fault.

We brainstormed a list of solutions and decided to try one that didn't focus on punishment but instead provided us with a tool for making positive change. We worked together to create a chart for our wall. One side of the chart had disrespectful phrases on it, such as *shut up*. We discussed why a student would say "shut up" to another student: What would prompt it? What could the speaker be feeling? We then thought of other, kinder phrases students could use to convey what they meant to say: "I really need to concentrate right now. Do you mind working at a different table?" Or even, "I don't like that. Please stop."

Once the chart was posted, students could refer to it when they felt the urge to use hurtful language. For a while, that meant that I needed to remind them to refer to the poster when I heard them lashing out. But after a week or two, they began to do it on their own, even reminding each other, "Go to the chart!"

After a few weeks, the problem had deescalated considerably. I believe that this was mostly because students were in charge of both identifying and solving the issue. The other important component was that they had a time and a place to really explore the cause of the behavior without feeling shamed or singled out. This was not just one person's problem; we approached it and solved it as a community.

Adapted from the blog post "Class Meetings Build Community, Safe Zone" (www.tolerance.org/blog/class-meetings-build-community-safe-zone) and reprinted with permission of Teaching Tolerance, a project of the Southern Poverty Law Center.

TEACH COLLABORATION

Collaboration is yet another "lifeworthy" skill necessary in the civic classroom. Place-based learning is not about working independently or in isolation. When students undertake large, interdisciplinary projects, they need to operate as a team, both as a class and in small groups. The class is working toward a common goal, so the work becomes a team effort.

We often ask students to collaborate, but we don't always remember that kids need instruction on how to do it. How many times have we seen one student carry the workload for others, or a small group dissolve into argument and chaos, or continually engage in off-task behavior? Sometimes we even see these things happen when adults work together, because collaboration can be hard! So what can we do to scaffold more successful and educational experiences for our students?

We need to teach kids how to work together. Here are a few tools and other ideas for teaching students how to collaborate on tasks and projects:

- Role play: Have students brainstorm scenarios where they have had problems working in small groups. Students act out skits demonstrating the issues and ask the class for ideas on how to address the problems. Then the actors try them out. This can be done during a class meeting or over a few days in the beginning of the school year.
- Make a problem-solving book for the classroom: This is similar to the role play idea, but instead of acting, students create comic strips showing the problem followed by a list of possible solutions. The book stays in the classroom as a resource throughout the year as problems arise.
- Assign jobs: Many times group work fails because the lack of structure is scary for students; they just don't know what to do. One way to alleviate their anxiety is to give each student within a group a clearly defined role. Jobs can include facilitator, timekeeper, recorder, illustrator, and data collector, or you can give each student a specific research question to answer. It's a good idea to have students practice with the different roles before jump-

ing into a real project; it is also important to make sure the jobs rotate so that the same students are not always doing the same things.

- Examine group dynamics: We have all watched students fall into familiar patterns when working with others. There is one who usually checks out, one who becomes the distractor, one who scolds and threatens. Students can begin to break these patterns when they have more self-awareness. Talking to students about group dynamics can initiate a discourse and offer the class a common vocabulary.

- Reflect, reflect, reflect: Make sure that both you and the students see group work itself as part of the learning experience. Leave time at the end of each session for reflection, either written or conversational. Even the most basic check-in questions can offer students insight and make them feel heard: What went well? What did not go well? What can your group do differently next time? What can you do differently next time? Couching these questions within a larger discussion of group dynamics and team member responsibilities can go a long way toward teaching students about themselves and how they work with others.

- Accountability: Students and parents often complain about group work because they feel it is unfair. If one student performs poorly, it can negatively affect their team members' grade. As much as possible, give each individual student their own personal score on a group project. Also, make sure that the final grade values process, not just product, like giving each student daily points based on how they fulfilled their role during class time. This also communicates to students that you, their teacher, are paying attention and that how they act and function in a group is important to you, their team members, and the class.

- Community-building: All of the other components of creating a healthy, collaborative classroom will help with group work. The more kids know and appreciate one another, the easier it can be to work together.

Once students have accumulated tools for working with their classmates, they can practice these skills when working with people and partners in the community. Learning to collaborate gives students the means to successfully participate in an effort that is larger than themselves, and hones a skill that is valuable in higher education, careers, and civic life.

GIVE STUDENTS A VOICE

In order for our students to be truly invested in their classroom, they need to feel ownership over both content and process. Student input means that kids will naturally be more interested in completing quality work because they have more of a stake in the outcome. Incorporating student voice in place-based projects allows young people to have a direct impact on the community. When we encourage kids to speak up and add their voices to the public forum, we are training future citizens who will actively participate in their democracy.

Some of the practices already referenced in this chapter demonstrate how student voice can be integrated into the classroom. Class meetings are one of the most powerful avenues for doing this. Giving students a leadership role in problem-solving can lend itself well to other aspects of the curriculum. There are often many points within a project when the class needs to decide what to do next. This is a great time to introduce different types of voting such as majority, two-thirds majority, and consensus, so that students can practice with more than just one way of coming to a group decision.

The first few weeks of school are the time when teachers and students can work together to create classroom norms. Some teachers call these norms rules, whereas others call them agreements. Middle or high school teachers might even consider making parallels between classroom rule-making and the Constitution. The preamble offers a helpful structure for the class to emulate. Students can substitute their own words for the privileges and services listed by the Founding Fathers. The class could also draft its own Bill of Rights, and perhaps the teacher could create one, too. The overall goal is for students to have a hand in establishing the norms of their classroom community.

In some cases it may work out for students to choose the projects they work on. If teachers give them the tools to observe and assess their communities, a class may be able to identify problem areas and work to propose solutions. This is especially possible with older grades. The guide Healthy Neighborhoods, Healthy Kids from Shelburne Farms (introduced in chapter 2) lays out a wonderful curriculum for assessing neighborhoods with kids of all ages.[4]

It is not always feasible for students to have a say in choosing topics because place-based projects are often dictated by the needs of partner organizations. But in these cases, there can still be room for students to choose how they contribute to the final product. Maybe an agency wants the class to develop a tool to help disseminate information, but the class can propose the format. Or perhaps there are several different jobs required, such as writer, illustrator, statistician, or builder, and individuals can apply for the role that suits them best.

Reflection and feedback are other valuable ways for students to have a voice in the classroom. By asking students what they most enjoyed about a project, what was the most challenging, and what advice they would give for the next time, we are letting them in on our teaching process and giving them a well-deserved role in formulating future curriculum.

While it is imperative that we give students a voice, it is also unrealistic for classrooms to be entirely democratic, especially in elementary and middle schools. Teachers are ultimately still in charge, and our leadership is necessary to guide students through difficult conflicts and sensitive situations, never mind required curricular content. We set the tone, introduce new ideas and systems when needed, and redirect potentially harmful discussions and behaviors. But generally, ceding some of our control to the students can be a powerful step toward building a community based on mutual respect and engaged learning.

Fostering a group of students who can work together, problem-solve, listen to others, and confidently contribute to the running of the community is a teacher's dream come true. Most of us work toward this ideal in order to establish and maintain healthy classroom relationships. In a place-based school, however, the skills outlined in this chapter are essential tools students need to be ready for civic engagement. The more we can help our young people gain fluency in these areas, the better we are preparing them to take an active role in their communities and in our democracy.

RESOURCES

Some of the best resources for creating community in the classroom are the Responsive Classroom books The First Six Weeks of School (2015) and The Morning Meeting Book (2014) by Roxann Kriete and Carol Davis. The First Six Weeks is written for elementary school teachers but can easily be adapted for middle school students. There may be some helpful ideas for high school teachers, as well.

Guidebooks for leading class meetings in your classrooms include Positive Discipline in the Classroom: Developing Mutual Respect, Cooperation, and Responsibility in Your Classroom (2013) and Positive Discipline: A Teacher's A-Z Guide, both by Jane Nelsen, Lynn Lott, and H. Stephen Glenn.

Teaching Tolerance's "Mix It Up at Lunch Day" is a great way to bring civic action to the social scene in the cafeteria. http://www.tolerance.org/mix-it-up/what-is-mix

Teaching Tolerance has also published an online handbook for teaching civil discourse in the classroom. http://www.tolerance.org/handbook/civil-discourse-classroom/civil-discourse-classroom

"No Name-Calling Week" resources from GLSEN include lesson plans, activities, and discussion topics to help kids tackle issues around bigotry and uncivil discourse in their schools. https://www.glsen.org/nonamecallingweek

NOTES

1. Shuster, Kate. 2017. Civil Discourse in the Classroom and Beyond. Teaching Tolerance. Accessed May 21, 2017. http://www.tolerance.org/publication/chapter-1-civil-discourse-classroom-and-beyond.
   2. Ibid.

3. Nelsen, Jane, Lynn Lott, and H. Stephen Glenn. 2013. Positive Discipline in the Classroom: Developing Mutual Respect, Cooperation, and Responsibility in Your Classroom. 4th ed. New York: Three Rivers Press.

4. Morra, Ryan, Holly Brough, and Jen Cirillo, eds. 2015. Healthy Neighborhoods, Healthy Kids Guide. Shelburne, VT: Shelburne Farms' Sustainable Schools Project.

Partnerships as Opportunity: Natural Segues into Learning

Partnerships are a key element of place-based education; they are what connect the students to the greater community. But how are these relationships built? How do we find them? What strategies can we use to make them successful?

No two partnerships are the same. This makes the cultivation of school-community relationships exciting, but it is also a lot of work. However, just as all relationships with cooperating organizations are different, so are the ways we can pursue them depending on time and resources.

At the Cottonwood School, we talk a lot about our connections to other organizations and agencies, but the truth is that we are referring to different levels of working relationships. We may partner with an agency for one project only or we may work with them year after year. Sometimes we contact an organization, business, or agency with curricular content in mind and sometimes we reach out to start the conversation before knowing how we will work together, if at all.

WHAT IS A "PARTNERSHIP"?

In a *Clearing* magazine article, Pat Willis from Oregon State University Extension Education Center describes partnerships this way: "A partnership is not just a cash donation, a one-time guest speaker, or a guided field trip. It starts with a conversation and it is participatory. All parties must benefit from the partnership, and at its best, society at large should be enriched. Healthy partnerships are long-lasting, goal driven, and must be enjoyable."[1]

It is essential that we recognize all the dynamics at play within school-community relationship building. As Willis points out, a field trip does not a partnership make. Good partnerships are built to last and must be mutually beneficial—similar to a healthy relationship between two people. They require attention, consideration, and reflection. All of this takes time.

As we have developed our program at the Cottonwood School, learning how to work with organizations, agencies, and businesses has been an experiential process. The word *partnership* is not very specific; there are many types of relationships that fall under its umbrella. In struggling to define these different affiliations, we have found that it is at least helpful to sort them into two general categories: short-term and long-term.

Our short-term partners are groups we work with on only one project, usually over a trimester. Most of these relationships are cultivated in response to a curricular need. For example, our 7th and 8th graders were planning to study forestry, so we contacted Portland's Urban Forestry Department to see how we could work together. Meanwhile, the 4th and 5th graders were studying watersheds, so we contacted our local watershed council.

Short-term partnerships often do not require much time commitment from the partner. They usually involve an initial meeting or two, an introductory visit to the classroom, and a presentation at the end of the project. There may be one more school visit added for a representative to give feedback to students during the process.

We approach our long-term partners differently. We identify organizations and agencies with similar goals or interests or because they share our neighborhood—it is useful to note that most nonprofit organizations are required to work with the community as part of their mission. We start these relationships with a conversation about our mutual needs, find overlaps, and develop curricular ties accordingly. We work with these groups over an array of projects and grade levels and support these relationships with documents such as partnership agreements and volunteer positions.

The status of a partnering organization can easily shift and change. Some of our short-term partners become long-term when we repeat a curricular unit over several years. We also hope that by inviting community members and experts into our school and classrooms, we are sowing the seeds for potential partnerships in the future.

HOW TO FIND PARTNERS

Partnerships are our bridge to the wider community. In terms of connection, it is helpful to think about what Pat Willis calls "access points" when we set out to find partners:

> Perhaps the most critical skills we need to develop to create and maintain successful partnerships are being able to identify access points within the community. An access point can be as simple as a well asked question, a community need, or a community change. It may be born trying to solve a local problem or seeking information that doesn't yet exist. An access point can be any project or place or set of societal or environmental conditions which allow or promote community engagement to meet a need.[2]

There are several approaches you can take to find these access points— some systematic, some exploratory—and it often makes sense to combine them.

In his book *Place-Based Education*, David Sobel suggests ways for schools to strategically connect with the broader community and build a school-sponsored place-based program. His first suggestion is to "put an environmental educator in every school."[3] This person, often in a part-time position, provides support and expertise in both environmental science and local history, acts as an outreach coordinator, communicates and documents program details and highlights to the community, and helps teachers craft place-based curricular units.[4]

At the Cottonwood School, we were able to create such a position seven years after opening, once we could establish funding to support it. The fieldwork and place-based education coordinator job description includes all of the tasks outlined by Sobel. It has been integral in our mission as a place-based school. The coordinator helps train new teachers in place-based education and mentors them as they create their first curriculums. Having someone research, coordinate fieldwork, and reach out to partners is an incredible support to teachers who are already maxed out on time.

Sobel also suggests planning and holding Community Vision to Action Forums. These are meetings that include people from all parts of a community to identify "what they love about their community and what challenges they face. Then, after a process of prioritization, action committees are formed to address the three to five most salient issues."[5] Projects then emerge from this prioritized list.

We haven't yet held a Community Vision to Action Forum at the Cottonwood School, but it is something we would like to do. This only goes to show that you don't have to start with a big-picture strategic plan with potential partners, although it is a great way to ground your program in the intention and practice of meeting community needs.

One of the most important things to remember when approaching and beginning a relationship with an organization, agency, or other group is that all projects and outcomes should be mutually beneficial. To this end, it is helpful to learn as much as you can about the mission, goals, and history of your potential partner, and to be ready to share all these things about your school.

Administrators, teachers, and parent volunteers can look for opportunities while also planting seeds by attending neighborhood association meetings and watershed council meetings and signing up for newsletters from local science museums and historical societies. Getting involved with organizations and groups before you ask them to work together is a great way to both "feel them out" and build trust.

LONG-TERM PARTNERS

One of the longest-lasting partnerships we have nurtured is with a retirement community six blocks away. Our students interact with the residents in a myriad of ways across grade levels:

- Kindergarteners visit on Halloween to trick-or-treat in the assisted living unit and in December to make holiday ornaments.
- 1st and 2nd graders visit once a month to meet with a group of residents who have committed to being their "reading buddies."
- 7th and 8th grade students participate in service internships where they volunteer in the building one afternoon a week for eight weeks; as part of this program, students have helped run activities

in the memory care unit, worked as aides in the library, and served as technology tutors for residents needing help with their phones, tablets, or computers.

- Residents have also hosted art shows featuring student work, hosted celebrations such as the Stone Soup communal feast before Thanksgiving, and provided a panel of World War II veterans to speak with our 7th and 8th graders.

Both partner organizations benefit from this relationship. Students have access to a wealth of life experience and the residents are able to mentor and enjoy the students. Both have gained an attentive audience. Connecting people across generations can help increase understanding and compassion for the "other." It can also help bring a neighborhood closer together. Before we worked with this retirement home, most of the residents didn't even know our school existed. Now residents recognize our students when we are out for neighborhood walks and stop to say hello (photo 7.1).

Photo 7.1.   *Resident from a local retirement home reads with two 1st and 2nd graders.*
Photo by Nesa Levy

Building this partnership was neither easy nor fast. We built it piece by piece, starting several years ago with just one project. Part of the difficulty lay in the size of the retirement community. The building is 30 floors high, and most of the residents are in the independent living section. This means that there is not an activity director or other centralized staff member with whom to coordinate or contact. Residents form their own interest groups that function separately from the administration of the facility. When approaching such a large organization, it is often tough to find an entry point.

The memory care unit was a good place for us to start because there is an activity director assigned to the wing. The director was also excited and willing to work with us. During the first three years we partnered with the retirement community, we sent a small group of middle school students to volunteer once a week as part of our service internship program. After three years, we had built up enough goodwill with the activity director (and enough confidence in our own program) to reach out beyond the memory care unit. This also coincided with the development of our fieldwork coordinator position.

A resident services specialist helped us put an email out asking if anyone would be interested in a Reading Buddies program. She set up a time for us to meet with the few people who responded. When we walked into the meeting, expecting to talk with two or three residents, we were surprised to find a group of 20–25 people with eager smiles.

The group of residents had a lot of questions for us. What is our school's mission? What are our demographics? What is a charter school? We spent most of the time fielding these questions while also hearing about how much these people wanted to work with children. Many of them had a background in teaching or education. Some of them had a skill, like quilt-making or woodworking, that they wanted to share. It was exciting to know that such a valuable resource existed right down the street from us.

Our 1st and 2nd grade Reading Buddies program grew out of that original meeting. Two years later, one of the residents who had been most active in the program proposed the creation of a volunteer "liaison" position to serve as a communication and organizational link between the retirement community and our school. The liaison helps to coordinate events throughout the year, makes sure that room reservations are made with the resident services office, and recruits partici- pants within the community. This has been a tremendous support to further strengthen the partnership between our two organizations.

This relationship, however, depends on whether there will be a resi- dent interested in and willing to take on a leadership position. Many partnerships rely on individuals within organizations who have the interest and impetus to maintain them. If that person leaves, it could have a significant impact. One effort we have made toward alleviating this problem is crafting partnership agreement documents.

We have been most successful in using partner agreements within our Adopt-a-Place program. Each of our six grade levels has "ad- opted" a park, greenspace, or natural area not far from the school. Each class visits their place at least six times over the course of the year. Two of these visits must be service-related (photo 7.2). We coordinate the service work with the agencies that manage each par- ticular place. For most of the properties, that agency is Portland Parks and Recreation.

Photo 7.2.   Two 6th-grade students pull invasive English ivy at Tryon Creek State Park, their adopted place.
Photo by Robin McAdoo

When we first began this program, we designed a "Partnership Agreement Form" to help articulate our goals, plan the projects, and agree on responsibilities (see figure 7.2 at the end of the chapter). The document has a section for both the school and the partner to articulate goals and commitments. It also has two-year timeline of service projects, which is created in conjunction with Portland Parks ecologists.

The agreements have been incredibly helpful, especially in years when there has been a high staff turnover rate in the parks department. By referring to the documents, we don't have to start rebuilding the partnership from the beginning; we simply pick up where we left off. The agreements are not the same as a legal contract, but they do help to maintain a level of commitment between our school and the partnering agency while also outlining the terms of our relationship.

The Adopt-a-Place program is another example of a mutually beneficial long-term partnership. The parks department receives more than 400 hours of volunteer service a year from the school. In exchange, our students have the opportunity to learn more about the natural areas where they live. If a student attends our school for all nine years, they will leave with stronger connections in at least five natural areas in our city.

We have also designed the program so that the kindergarteners and the 7th and 8th graders share the same natural area. This offers opportunities for the older students to mentor the younger ones during tree-planting, mulching, and other service days. Additionally, it allows kindergarteners to come back to the same place seven years later and see how their service made a lasting impact. The habitat they worked to restore now hosts salamanders and native frogs! We hope that by seeing these achievements firsthand, students will be inspired to perform more environmental service in the future.

NATURAL PARTNERSHIPS

All students learn about watersheds when they learn about the water cycle, ecology, and the impact of humans on the earth. When we began designing our unit for the 4th and 5th grades, we knew that we wanted students to somehow see different parts of a watershed, starting from the higher elevation, moving to the stream that gathers water from that area, and following it to the water's destination near the ocean.

Since we are between the Cascade Mountains and the Pacific Ocean, our first thought was to start the exploration somewhere on Mt. Hood, a Cascadian volcano about an hour from Portland. We could go to the headwaters of a stream, then visit one of the larger rivers that flows from the foothills of the mountain into the mighty Columbia River and ultimately into the ocean. Students would visit each of these streams and rivers, study maps, and understand a watershed firsthand.

After some more thought about the logistics behind this unit and how far we would need to travel, we decided to look a little closer to home. This decision turned out to be a good one. We started by looking at a relationship we had already cultivated. Our 6th graders regularly visit their adopted place, Tryon Creek State Park, situated only a few miles from school. The park offers a well-developed series of environmental education classes for elementary students led by naturalists, including one about watersheds. This seemed like a logical place to start, especially since many of our students live in the Tryon Creek watershed.

Tryon Creek runs into the Willamette River, the main waterway in Portland, which flows only a few hundred feet from our school. Planning a trip to the state park and a walking field trip to the Willamette on another day covered two points on the water's journey to the Pacific.

The other obvious choice was to set up a field trip to the Columbia River Maritime Museum in Astoria, Oregon, close to where the river meets the ocean. Since this is a considerable distance from the school, it made sense to schedule this trip at the end of the trimester as a culminating event.

We could have left the "hands-on" fieldwork at that. Three points of contact is pretty good! But we still had questions about the local leg of the route. Where does Tryon Creek begin, anyway? And where does it meet the Willamette?

We called the visitor center at the state park to answer our question about the headwaters. The person on duty referred us to the volunteer coordinator for the Tryon Creek Watershed Council (TCWC), so we sent an email with the same question.

The following conversations yielded lots of new information. We learned that Tryon Creek begins in the area around an apartment complex in the Portland neighborhood of Multnomah Village. As the TCWC representative explained, a lot of people imagine the headwaters of creeks and rivers to be in pristine, remote wilderness areas (as with our visions of the Cascadian headwaters). But Tyron Creek is an urban river and its source is in an urban area. What a great reminder that "nature" and city are not two separate entities!

With a little more digging, we found out that the apartment complex built near the headwaters (fittingly called "The Headwaters") was codesigned with the City of Portland's Bureau of Environmental Services (BES) as a model for ecologically sustainable building. We contacted the volunteer coordinator at BES since we had worked with her before to see what she knew. Since she had not worked with BES long, she had never heard of this place, but she was interested and offered to investigate.

A few weeks later, our BES contact called back saying that she had visited and talked to the property manager. She offered to guide a field trip to the complex and lead a scavenger hunt where students would work in groups to take photos of sustainable design features such as rain gardens and native plantings. This was a great opportunity; it wasn't a prefabricated field trip offered by BES and it fit our program perfectly. We would not have found this option without some investigation of our own, and it never would have happened without a willing partner in the cooperating agency.

But the real heart of our watershed unit came to us when we learned more about the confluence of Tryon Creek and the Willamette River. Before the creek meets the river, it runs under Highway 43 through a 400-foot long culvert. This culvert is so long that salmon and other native fish species cannot make it through. The engineers who designed the highway and constructed the culvert in the 1920s certainly did not have fish in mind.

Removing the culvert is at the center of many efforts made by TCWC. They had even made a short film to educate people about the negative impact it has on the ecosystem. We learned that a plan is being proposed to replace the culvert with an overpass, as part of a civil engineering project.

Here is where opportunity naturally presented itself. We found a story and a real reason for students to learn about watersheds in the place where ecology, civics, and activism overlapped. We asked if there was anything we could do to help and the answer was "Yes! Absolutely!" And a partnership was formed.

We visited the culvert with the TCWC representative and planned a visit for the students. We talked about options for the students to take on a letter-writing campaign or to build a website educating people about the issue. According the TCWC, a lot of people don't even know what a culvert is. We received blueprints for the Army Corps of Engineers plan, which could help students build their own model. There were so many possibilities within this project for learning across the curriculum while at the same time providing TCWC with valuable material. This was definitely a win-win situation.

The path to our partnership with TCWC started with a curricular need. This is different from the more systematic method of starting with community needs. Because we strive to develop place-based units on all grade levels multiple times a year, we often start the search for partners by looking at our curriculum map. By putting in the time to more deeply investigate local connections to curricular content, we more often than not uncover an organization or agency that is a natural fit for partnership. Through this process, we also gain knowledge and

Preparing Students and Partners to Work Together

Most of the following tips are adapted from the video *Building School/ Community Partnerships* from the University of Michigan–Flint *Discovering Place* video series: https://www.umflint.edu/outreach/discovering-place-video-2.

To prepare the students:

- Brief students on how to interact with adults. If necessary, lead mini-lessons.
- Give students background information on your partner's agency or organization before they meet a representative.

- Lead a lesson that explicitly links classroom content to the partner's project so that students are clear on how and why we are working together.
- Impress upon your students the need for high-quality work (and allow them time to achieve it). Unreliable, low-quality work can jeopardize the partnership.

To prepare the partners:

- Be considerate of the time of day when a partner visits; help navigate the school's visitor policy.
- Manage your class and help facilitate engagement.
- Offer your partner a cheat sheet on how to present to students, including basic tips on how to encourage student participation and incorporate hands-on learning.
- Discuss activities ahead of time to ensure appropriateness.
- Discuss logistics and how you will work together, whether on a single field trip or a long-term partnership.
- Help partners to learn about the educational needs of students.
- If necessary, clearly communicate that classes operate on strict schedules; time overages may create issues.
- During and after the project: Thank your partner, publicly support your partner when possible, and have students write thank-you notes.

"expertise" on the topic, just as teachers transition into the position of historian when learning about local history.

BEING "OPPORTUNITY-MINDED"

Sometimes we stumble upon a new project and partnership as a by-product of doing real work in the community.

Several years ago, our middle school students were conducting research at a local park in an effort to gain "heritage tree" status for a stand of Oregon white oaks. This was something the Parks Department had on their back burner for years. They handed it over to us since our students used the park regularly and had taken a keen interest in the resident squirrels. As part of the project, students learned how to take tree measurements from a forester so that they could report the data on the application. They also learned the basics of tree identification, the history of the property, and how animals and people use and have historically used Oregon white oaks.

Once we completed our application, compiled our research, and even created an oral presentation, we looked for people and organizations who would write letters of support. In the summer, the Oregon Electric Railway Historical Society (OERHS) operated an electric trolley on the tracks that run among the grove of trees. We thought they would have an interest in preserving the oaks and maintaining undeveloped property along the trolley line. We decided to ask the OERHS for a letter.

However, the OERHS wrote back and said they could not support our application. The regional government was in the middle of a campaign to turn the defunct railroad line into an electric streetcar line for commuters coming from south of the city. The OERHS did not want to do anything that would compromise that effort.

Because none of the teachers who work at our school live along that set of railroad tracks or in the suburban towns south of the city, we were not aware of this campaign. Over the summer, we worked to establish a connection within the regional government (which took several months) and landed on a deal. They would help us get an "inside look" into the streetcar line planning, and we would turn our learnings into educational podcasts that they would post on their website. Since the proposed line was turning out to be controversial, the agency representatives thought that the student voice would show a softer side of the project and overall be good PR.

The forthcoming unit stretched over a year and covered several content areas. Students studied primary and secondary documents telling the history of streetcars in Portland (which turns out to be quite rich!), and wrote radio skits about some of the more interesting stories. We met with the owner and director of the only streetcar manufacturing company in the United States and built scale models of the streetcars using blueprints from the company (photo 7.3). We also met with a representative from the regional government who explained how they predict future traffic patterns and plan public transportation routes, which students also turned into an entertaining podcast.

This project never would have happened if we hadn't written that one request to the OERHS, or if they hadn't answered. It also wouldn't have happened if we didn't see their rejection of our request as an opportunity.

Photo 7.3.   Studying Portland Streetcar blueprints in preparation for building a scale model.
Photo by author

Being opportunity-minded is a critical skill when designing place-based units and place-based schools. Sometimes we discover project ideas and potential partnerships just by reading the local newspaper, or meeting someone new at a social gathering. You never know when an opportunity will present itself.

One entry point into partnership is the land itself. In the example of the Oregon white oak trees, we established the project with Portland Parks and Recreation because our students had developed an interest in the property. Pat Willis and Susan Cross explore how this approach can be student-led in their article "Starting a Community-Based Natural Resource Education Program":

> After you determine what site or sites you may be able to use for your program you will need to find out as much as possible about the site. In an ideal situation, this entire process can be done by your students. You will want to find out who owns the property. Who is in charge of managing it? Can you use the site as a study center? Are there special things about the site? Is it a protected area? How will you minimize the impact of your student's [sic] presence at the site? Get maps of the local area. Talk to homeowners associations and neighborhood businesses. Can you do enhancement work there? How could the site be improved for wildlife or educational uses? What kind of information would it be useful to have about the site? Who might best use that information? What is the history of the site? Are there any cultural values?[6]

Involving your students in the process of investigation and community outreach will not only increase the ownership they feel over the project, but also give them tremendous hands-on experience with numerous career skills.

Not all partnerships will be successful. Sometimes the "perfect" agency for the project doesn't have the time or resources to work with you. Sometimes you will find a partner who is eager and willing, but you can't find a project that is mutually beneficial or would interest the students. We have had the most challenges trying to partner with large agencies or organizations such as statewide science centers or the medical university down the street. It can be hard to find an entry point. In these situations, it is often a matter of waiting until we can find someone with connections who can get us in the door. But even that does not always work.

Entry Points into Partnerships

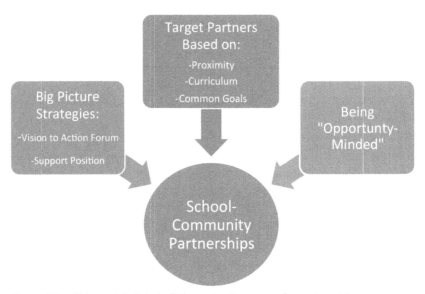

Figure 7.1.   Entry points into building school–community partnerships.

When you conduct initial conversations with potential partners, you can usually get a feeling for whether it is a good fit. It may be a red flag if the person you meet with seems overly anxious about committing time or resources, or if the concept of place-based education doesn't strike a chord. Noncommunicative partners also may not be worth your time. As a school, your time and resources are already limited; you need to find a partner who will at least meet you partway.

Overall, we have found that just as there is more than one type of partnership, there are many ways to find partners (figure 7.1). The best approach is to use multiple strategies: holding a Community to Vision Action Forum; reaching out to organizations, agencies, and businesses in your neighborhood; investigating specific curricular topics and looking for local connections; and, above all, just keeping your eyes and ears open. Once you get into the habit of seeing the community as your classroom, opportunities for partnerships will present themselves all around you.

School and Community Partner Agreement

School Name	Organization/Community Partner	
School Contact/Title	Partner Contact/Title	
Mailing Address	Mailing Address	
Phone	Email	Phone	Email
School Leader	Partner Leader	

Partnership Start Date: End Date: Annual Review Date:

The vision of this school-community partnership:

Shared Partner Goals:

Partner Goal(s):
Partner Commitments/Responsibilities:

Figure 7.2.   Example of a School–Community Partner Agreement Form.

School Goal(s):

School Commitments/Responsibilities:

Estimated # of hours

Estimated # of students impacted:

We agree to a partnership which will enhance and improve the quality of education and meet the needs of the students and educators as well as the needs of the partner organization and community members. We agree to partnership activities and responsibilities, to review progress and partner status on an annual basis, and any mutually agreed upon changes to the partner agreement.

Parties should attach a completed one-year calendar of agreed upon activities.

SIGNATURES

_____

School Partner- Printed name and signature   Date

_____

Community Partner- Printed name and signature   Date

Figure 7.2.   Continued.

RESOURCES

The University of Michigan–Flint created a video series called *Discovering Place* about how to implement place-based education. The 35-minute installment on building partnerships offers lots of tips from the point of view of both the school and partnering agencies. https://www.umflint.edu/outreach/discovering-place-watch-videos

Learning to Make Choices for the Future: Connecting Public Lands, Schools, and Communities through Place-Based Learning and Civic Engagement by Delia Clark (2008) contains a chapter entitled "Building Strong Community Partnerships." Within are tips from teachers, advice for creating a common vision, and real-world examples. The appendix also provides a helpful worksheet to use when initiating a conversation with a potential partner.

NOTES

1. Willis, Pat. 2014. "Strategies for Community-Based Education: Developing Healthy Partnerships." *Clearing*, January 2. http://clearingmagazine.org/archives/9056.

2. Ibid.

3. Sobel, David. 2013. *Place-Based Education: Connecting Classrooms and Communities*. Great Barrington, MA: The Orion Society, 74.

4. Ibid.

5. Ibid, 78.

6. Willis, Patrick, and Susan Cross. 2014. "Starting a Community-Based Natural Resource Education Program." *Clearing*, June 13. http://clearingmagazine.org/archives/10042.

CHAPTER 8

Empathy, Play, and Place-Based Education in the Primary Grades

In the primary grades, children are learning how to learn. For most children, however, this is not something they have to be taught because they are already hardwired for it through the act of play. Research has shown that play is how young students develop communication, cognitive, and socioemotional skills. Through play children demonstrate curiosity, solve problems, regulate emotions, and resolve conflicts.[1] All of these skills—and the many more that are honed through the process of play—will be necessary as children grow up in a place-based, civically active school environment.

The traditional classroom tends not to support young students' inclination toward play. But based on how children naturally learn, asking a kindergartener or 1st grader to sit most of the day and do worksheets or memorize facts is counterproductive. By allowing our students to explore the places where they live through both hands-on and imaginative play, we create an engaging—and developmentally appropriate—educational alternative for primary students.

A student's love for the place where they live starts with time in the field exploring parks, forests, buildings, and streets. In the younger elementary grades (K–3), children are developmentally geared for hands-on, experiential education and are most interested in learning about the here and now.[2] Although some educators feel that place-based education is better suited for middle school, high school, and older students, we have found that it is perfectly aligned to the needs and interests of our youngest scholars.

David Sobel outlines three distinct stages of child development in relationship to environmental education: connection, investigation, and action.[3] In the connection stage, young children play, explore, and pretend in nature. This helps them build empathy and a feeling of belonging in the natural world.

In the next stage, middle grade children begin to learn more about their environment through research and other investigations. This is when children may be able to apply what they know about the environment near them to places farther away.

In the action stage, older students learn more about problems or conflicts, such as pollution or deforestation, and propose courses of action for change. By the time children are in late elementary school or middle school, they have built a strong connection to the environment and therefore care enough to want to protect it. The aim is that their love for nature will be stronger than their fear of or for it, combating the risk of disconnection.[4]

Sobel suggests that if we are not conscious of these stages when teaching about our environment, we lose the opportunity to create strong bonds between our children and their place. If we focus on big environmental concerns too early, we run the risk of turning our kids off from environmental studies by overwhelming them with doom and gloom.[5]

We honored this perspective of children's developmental growth when we planned our school-wide curriculum map at the Cottonwood School. Our K–2 curriculum is very much rooted in what is most relevant in a young student's life: family, school, neighborhood, and local environment. Place-based education at this age focuses on immersion in the environment, pretend play, and the introduction of problem-solving skills. Service has a place in some curricular units, but is not incorporated as much as in older grades. Third grade acts as a bridge between the younger and the intermediate grades.

KINDERGARTEN: THE POND STUDY

During spring, our kindergarteners focus their attention on one place: Oaks Bottom Wildlife Refuge in Southeast Portland. The refuge, located near the east bank of the Willamette River, is a floodplain wetland and one of the only remaining swaths of marshland in Portland. The land is home to blue herons, deer, salamanders, and much more wildlife. Luckily, the city decided to purchase this property in 1969 before it was developed into an industrial park.[6]

It is easy to forget that you are in a city when visiting the 141-acre refuge. Trails wind down the bluff from the Sellwood neighborhood above through a forest of big-leaf maple and cedar. At the bottom, the land transitions from open meadow to marshland to oak forest. Hikers and birdwatchers are regaled with the chirps, squawks, and honks of both permanent and migratory residents.

Every week in April and May, our kindergarteners make the trek across the river to Oaks Bottom to explore, play, and learn. During their mornings in the refuge, students transition through three different stations: pond study, plant study, and play.

At the pond station, teacher Amanda McAdoo and parent volunteers teach children how to use nets to scoop up tadpoles and baby salamanders (called efts) and transfer them to large plastic tubs without hurting them. Students practice balancing on the rocks near the water's edge and observe the young amphibians. They learn the difference between a baby frog and a baby salamander, and for those who want to know more, simple taxonomy cards are available (photo 8.1).

Over the eight weeks they visit Oaks Bottom, students see the tadpoles transform. They also notice how the habitat changes from a saturated wetland to a smaller, more contained pond. These observations directly support lessons on the life cycle, seasons, and ecosystems. Through scaffolded activities and reflective conversations, Amanda helps students construct understandings built on their own hands-on experience.

In the plant station, students find and learn five to ten different native plants. Through stories and play, students discover the native, culinary, and medicinal uses of the local vegetation. Experiential learning helps students recognize and remember elderberry, snowberry, Oregon grape, black cottonwood, dogwood, licorice fern, sword fern, mock orange, piggyback plant, and salmonberry.

In the final station, the students have an opportunity to play with natural materials. Amanda prepares this area with several large sticks and small logs for the children to carry, stack, and build with. Groups

Photo 8.1.   A kindergartener investigates pond life.
Photo by Jeremy Weikel

often work together to create shelters, leading to imaginative and further cooperative play.

All of these stations are designed to teach the children about this
unique place in our city and help them connect with it. The focus isn't
just learning facts but learning a place because students visit Oaks
Bottom so many times. Exploring the pond and forest, and using the
environment as a playscape while making meaningful memories with
friends, is how we foster connection. It helps to make Oaks Bottom
a place students will remember and want to revisit. The refuge also
becomes a place they will want to protect, even if that recognition will
come later in their development.

As a culminating project for this two-month study a few years ago, students built a three-dimensional map of the refuge in their classroom. On one of their last visits, Amanda gave each of them a hand-drawn map of the area where they visited every week. She asked them to mark important features on the map as they walked through the area.

Back in the classroom, the students compared their maps and chose which features they wanted to include for their 3-D final version. Essential landmarks included the "Troll Bridge" (as coined by the class), the frog pond, pathways, and fences. Students also created small figurines of ducks, banana slugs, and other animals they saw in the refuge.

As a result of the wetlands study, most kindergartners could identify several native plants, were intimately familiar with pond ecology, and had a basic understanding of how to conduct a scientific investigation in the field. But more than this, they had learned about a new place to love (photo 8.2).

Photo 8.2.   Nature journaling in Oaks Bottom Wildlife Refuge.
Photo by Brittany Roska

1ST AND 2ND GRADES: STORYLINE AS A TEACHING STRATEGY

Walk into Nesa Levy's 1st and 2nd grade blended classroom and one of the first things you will notice is a large bulletin board covered with colorful paper. This visual display, called a frieze, depicts a specific location that changes with the unit of study. This trimester, the scene is of a neighborhood, complete with streets and buildings. The students have added details, built from shapes of cut painted paper, clay, and shoe boxes, like a multimedia collage.

For their unit—"What is a neighborhood?"—students brainstormed essential components, such as a hospital, a fire station, a grocery store, a post office, trees, and public transportation, and pasted them onto the original empty board. They also crafted characters who work in the neighborhood doing different jobs.

Building this artistic representation of what the students are learning is a central component of the Storyline model. Storyline, which originated in Scotland, gives a context for classroom curriculum by focusing on the elements of setting, characters, and events. The approach "uses the learners' enthusiasm for story-making" to make learning meaningful and memorable. The process integrates active learning and reflection while building on the students' existing experience and knowledge.[7]

The story creates a need and desire for the students to learn facts in order to move the plot forward. Holding a culminating celebration with community members, such as bringing in bus drivers and nurses after studying jobs in a neighborhood, fuses the story with the real world, indeed bringing the process to life. As with place-based education, this empowers students from a young age because they see how they're part of something bigger.[8]

As the Storyline website articulates, "The world is demanding more highly skilled workers who can problem-solve on their feet."[9] This is just one essential skill that our youngest students practice through a Storyline unit. Children also receive hands-on experience with collaboration, negotiation, learning to be flexible, and applying character traits—such as kindness and compassion—both in their story and toward their classmates.

Furthermore, the impetus for social and emotional development is stronger than in other types of project-based learning because the story exists in a larger context. Students develop empathy by imagining what it is like to be a real-life person from their community (a banker, a fire-fighter, a doctor), and they often receive feedback from people in those positions to help inform their assumptions.[10]

As students grow in our school, place-based projects tend to rely less on simulation, which is replaced by real-life situations. Storyline is a smart place to start. Children are given the opportunity to role-play in a safe and supportive environment while also learning essential information about our world and how to work with each other. To the kids, however, the entire process is really about play. The fun of building scenes and pretending to be characters is the true hook that allows for meaningful learning.

Storyline: Managing a Restaurant

Food culture is a defining aspect of Portland these days. Nesa and her partner teacher, Megan Richter, decided to concentrate on this aspect of our city for a trimester-long unit. Students didn't approach this topic from the point of view of a customer, however. In keeping with our goal of teaching valuable career skills and learning from experts in our community, the students examined restaurants through the perspective of the people who run them.

The teachers brainstormed a list of essential questions to guide their conversations with students: Why do we have restaurants? How do restaurants function? How do people choose where to eat? Where do restaurants get their food? How are restaurants different from one another? How do restaurants navigate decisions relating to cost, quality, and cuisine? How do restaurants deal with waste? What are the different jobs within a restaurant?

As part of their Storyline, the two classes had to decide what kind of restaurants to design and manage. One classroom chose to open a pizzeria, while the other class specialized in Mexican food. Based on students' knowledge of restaurants, each class created a frieze representing the features and layout of their establishment. Half of the frieze depicted the area where customers are served, and the other half represented the kitchen and storage areas.

The classes brainstormed a list of people who work in restaurants such as cooks, servers, hosts, and managers. Each student chose a role and crafted a paper representative of their character. They then journaled about their character and their duties in the restaurant.

Early in the unit, the head chef from a restaurant down the street came to speak to the classes. He gave the students an overview of his job and answered any questions they had.

A couple of weeks later, the chef invited the students into his restaurant before opening time to learn key vocabulary words, giving them firsthand experience with a working kitchen. They learned the difference between the "front of the house" and the "back of the house" and were able to interview a server. In the kitchen, the chef offered a baking demonstration so the students could see him in action and also learn how some of the equipment works.

From this visit the students were able to reassess their frieze and consider what might be missing. They discovered that they had forgotten to include a dishwasher. How would the dishes get washed without one? They all journaled on the conundrum and then decided to add a dishwasher to the frieze.

Next, both classes toured a different restaurant, this one owned and managed by the parents of a student. Again, the children saw the back of the house and asked questions. This time, they were also treated to a feast generously offered by the hosts.

The teachers challenged the students by asking, "What do restaurant managers do with leftover food? How do they deal with waste?" To answer this question, students traveled to a nearby food pantry. They helped carry produce and other food from a delivery van to the storage area. They also had a chance to interview the people who manage the pantry and learn how local restaurants and grocery stores can choose to contribute.

Back in the classroom, students discovered that they had received letters from "customers" (written by the teachers). Some patrons reported being very satisfied with their visit, while others lodged complaints. One diner commented that the service had been too slow and thus she might not be back. Nesa and Megan asked the students to journal some possible solutions to this problem. How could they speed up service?

After thinking and writing, the students came back with some great suggestions. One child recommended that they prep more food ahead of time. Another thought they could hire more chefs. And another proposed hanging a chalkboard in the kitchen to check off who had received their food so they could see who was still waiting.

To further link the unit to literacy, the teachers read aloud from the book *There's a Fly Guy in My Soup* by Todd Arnold to introduce a letter from a customer who had also found a fly in their food. Students again wrote and shared solutions to this problem.

For their final foray into the field, both classrooms signed up for a lesson at the Portland Culinary Workshop (PCW). Primarily designed for adults, the PCW offers classes in everything from proper knife use to Asian dumplings. The instructors led a two-hour workshop for the children on bread-making, which they decided would be the best fit for our age group. When students learned that they would be taking a baking class at a real culinary school, the announcement was followed by several minutes of cheering. In addition to making bread loaves at the workshop, students made cheesy breadsticks (photo 8.3).

Photo 8.3. Students make bread as part of the restaurant management unit.
Photo by Carrie Hartley

Both classes transformed their rooms into restaurants and hosted their families for a meal as a culminating project. To prepare for this event, our art teachers worked with students to make personalized aprons and ceramic food. Students from the pizzeria class molded mini-pizzas, and students from the Mexican restaurant class crafted tacos. Students also created menus, bills, and receipts, requiring them to practice skills in art, writing, and arithmetic.

On the grand opening day, students laid tablecloths and place settings in their rooms. They met to have a final check-in on what to do when people started to arrive. Once parents and grandparents were seated, students served their families pizza, donated by a local pizzeria, and cheese quesadillas, donated and made fresh on-site by cooks from the Mexican restaurant owned by one student's family. Although our school has limited resources for cooking since we don't have a kitchen, students did help make the tortillas on big cast iron grills set up outside.

Our 1st and 2nd graders rushed around, seating their family members, taking and delivering orders, and serving food. The challenges of being a restaurant server became clear. Nesa heard one student commenting on how tricky it was to remember who had ordered a quesadilla with cheese and who had ordered one without cheese, even after writing it down. Clearly, the job is more difficult than it looks, something the children would never know without doing it themselves. Through this shared experience, students may have even developed empathy for those in the service industry.

Running a restaurant was a natural hook for the kids. They had all experienced restaurants in one way or another, and pretending to cook and serve food is a common playtime activity. Connecting this preexisting interest with valuable skills and knowledge takes play to another level without the students even noticing.

Storyline: The Community Garden

Inspired by the science standards that ask students to learn about plants and basic botany, our 1st and 2nd grade teachers designed a Storyline around a community garden. Their classroom exploration coincided with hands-on experience in a real community garden in our neighborhood.

Guiding questions for this unit included the following: Why do people plant gardens? How can a garden help the local community? What are the parts of a plant? What do plants need to survive? What are the different uses for plants? How do people interact with plants? What is the growing season in the Pacific Northwest?

The classes created a frieze of a community garden. Through the process of figuring out what gardens need to grow, each child created a character with a job to help the plants. Once the plants and the characters were established in Storyline, students faced their first challenges.

One year, the garden had a thirsty plant problem. When students came into the classrooms one morning, they found thought bubbles next to plants on the frieze that said, "I'm thirsty!" The children needed to find ways to get water to the plants. They wrote about their proposed solutions: making a hose, making a watering can, making clouds and rain, or making a sprinkler.

Another year, the community garden frieze experienced an aphid infestation. The teachers punched holes in the plants and put white paper bugs everywhere. After researching possible solutions, the students decided to release ladybugs to eat the aphids. Each student created a ladybug, with correct insect body parts, and placed it in the garden. The aphid infestation subsided.

Meanwhile, the classes made several trips to the community garden four blocks away where we have two raised beds (photo 8.4). When they first visited in September, they were able to view a cornucopia of produce overflowing from members' plots. Since their own beds had been recently cleared by the teachers, the students had the opportunity to plant fall vegetables and tend to them on a weekly basis.

In addition to frequent fieldwork trips to the local garden, students also went to nearby Zenger Farm, a nonprofit teaching farm. There, students acquired direct experience with botany, soil science, nutrition, and farm chores. Students applied their knowledge about plant parts and performed the duties they had imagined in their Storyline.

At the end of the unit, students harvested plants from their garden plots. Using these vegetables, plus additional produce from home, students and their families worked together at school to make several batches of soup the week before Thanksgiving. The classes hosted a gathering open to all community gardeners, along with the students'

Photo 8.4.   A 1st grader explores the neighborhood community garden.
Photo by Nesa Levy

reading buddies from a local retirement home. Everyone brought their own bowl and spoon and enjoyed the meal while listening to a reading of the folktale *Stone Soup*. In past years, students opted to donate their harvest to a local food pantry.

School gardens have become common across the country. This unit is an easy way to link the garden to the curriculum while also extending connections to the broader community. Building the unit around story elements adds a sense of play that makes the learning even more relevant for young children.

3RD GRADE: BECOMING EXPERTS

At the Cottonwood School, the 3rd grade is intentionally on its own and not in a blend because the year serves as a bridge between the primary and intermediate grades. By the time students arrive at the 3rd grade, they are ready to apply play and problem-solving to large group projects that have a more direct impact on the community. They are also more prepared to think about the distant past and make even greater connections to professional careers.

One of our major units in the 3rd grade classroom is archaeology. Students study the ancient peoples who lived in this region while also learning *how* we learn about them. In this way, children can see how history is a process of investigation and inquiry, and not just a set of facts that have been handed to us.

We use the curriculum Project Archaeology, published by the State University of Montana in partnership with the Bureau of Land Management, as a guide through the first part of our unit. The lessons help students construct a solid understanding of this field of study. Two of the first questions are "What is archaeology and what does an archeologist do?" Students apply scientific concepts to their own lives and practice using terms such as *observation, inference, evidence, classification, category*, and *context*.

In recent years, students did not begin by learning about local native tribes. Instead, they learned how archaeologists use artifacts to understand the past by looking at tribes from regions all around the country. This gave the teacher a chance to cover basic North American regions and biomes. To complement the curriculum and learn more about local archeology, the class hosted a curator from the University of Oregon's Museum of Natural and Cultural History who gave a great introduction to artifacts and how we learn from them.

At the end of the continent-wide overview, students then had the opportunity to focus on one region, looking specifically at shelters built by native peoples. Our students learned about longhouses created by the Tsimshian tribe in coastal British Columbia. Classrooms from other regions of the United States who use Project Archaeology can choose a tribe closer to them.

Our 3rd graders continued their study by looking more closely at the Chinook tribe. They started at the Oregon Historical Society to view its exhibit on native peoples of Oregon. Students then traveled to the campus of Portland State University for a tour of the archaeology department led by a professor. This visit provided a direct link between the content students were learning and the profession of archaeology.

One of the highlights of the unit was a trip to the Ridgefield National Wildlife Refuge to see an authentic life-size replica of a Chinook longhouse, built on the site where a similar shelter once stood. Students went into the longhouse to see for themselves how the Chinook people slept, ate, gathered, and led their daily lives.

Back at school, the students turned their classroom into a longhouse by removing all chairs, pushing tables to the side, covering the walls with brown paper painted to look like cedar, and placing a "fire pit" in the center of the room. For a couple of weeks, all learning happened in this cozy, student-made longhouse.

This immersive aspect of the unit incorporated play into a very sophisticated study. It was a great way to extend the imaginative elements enjoyed in Storyline to the 3rd grade. Turning the classroom into a pretend longhouse was also a developmentally appropriate way for students this age to learn and build empathy for the people they were studying.

As described in the preface to this book, the class created an exhibit for Portland State University's Archaeology Roadshow in the spring as a culminating project. They were the only group of school-age children to present alongside scientists, professionals, and other experts (photo 8.5).

To prepare for this task, students visited the beloved Portland museum OMSI (Oregon Museum of Science and Industry) to help them think more carefully about how to build an engaging exhibit. They were able to go on a very special "behind the scenes" tour in the building where most of the exhibits are planned and built. Once back in the classroom, students listed all of the features of a "good" exhibit and began to plan how they could incorporate some of the elements into their own design.

The class decided to build a model longhouse, complete with interior details such as beds, bedding, food, and cooking tools. Next to the model, students created a sample area of land that showed how archaeologists identify historic longhouse sites. Hanging behind the model was a 3-D map of the western United States, highlighting the resources most utilized by native tribes. In front of the model, students placed a bucket of water and a tub of small cedar logs. The students encouraged visitors to place the cedar in the water and make guesses as to why the Chinook people chose this as their primary building material.

In addition to receiving the Archaeology Roadshow T-shirt, which went to all presenters, the students left with a feeling that they had contributed to something big—bigger than their classroom, bigger than our school, and bigger even than our neighborhood. Not only that, they were treated with respect by experts and were maybe even inspired to someday pursue a career in archaeology or a similar field in history or science.

Photo 8.5. A 3rd-grade student educates visitors at Portland State University's Archaeology Roadshow.
Photo by Amanda Mitchell

Young students' innate attraction to exploration and empathy makes place-based learning a perfect fit. Even at a young age, students appreciate and benefit from education that is authentic, relevant, and clearly connected to real life. By tapping into their desire to play and pretend, we create a safe environment to build myriad social and academic skills necessary for high-quality civic education. The rich experiences we provide our children through place-based explorations cultivate fertile ground for meaningful learning that will continue to influence their lives for years to come.

RESOURCES

The Storyline Design website offers background information about the method, plus additional resources and notices about trainings in the Pacific Northwest.
http://storyline.org/Storyline_Design/About_Us.html

The curricular guide *Project Archaeology: Investigating Shelter* is available for purchase on the program's website.
https://projectarchaeology.org/shop/investigating-shelter

For a comprehensive resource on play-based research, see *The Handbook of the Study of Play*, edited by James E. Johnson, Scott G. Eberle, Thomas S. Hendricks, and David Kuschner (2015).

NOTES

1. Heidemann, Sandra, and Deborah Hewitt. 2010. *Play: The Pathway from Theory to Practice*. St. Paul, MN: Redleaf Press.

2. Wood, Chip. 2007. *Yardsticks: Children in the Classroom Ages 4–14*. Turners Falls, MA: Center for Responsive Schools.

3. Sobel, David. 2013. *Beyond Ecophobia: Reclaiming the Heart in Nature Education*. Great Barrington, MA: The Orion Society.

4. Ibid.

5. Ibid.

6. City of Portland. "Oaks Bottom Wildlife Refuge." Accessed May 23, 2017. https://www.portlandoregon.gov/parks/finder/index.cfm?propertyid=490&action=ViewPark.

7. Storyline Design. "What Is the Storyline Method?" Accessed May 23, 2017. http://storyline.org/Storyline_Design/About_Us.html.

8. Levy, Nesa. Personal communication with author.

9. Storyline Design. "Integrating Curriculum." Accessed May 23, 2017. http://storyline.org/Storyline_Design/Articles_2.html.

10. Levy, personal communication.

CHAPTER 9

Middle School: Conflict, Service, and Active Citizenship

Middle school is a time of transition: from child to young adult, from more dependent to more independent, from elementary to high school. At this age, children's impulses pull them in different directions; they want to practice being grown-up, but they also want to be silly and have fun. This is a perfect time for students to have more hands-on experience in the world outside of the school building. They are eager to learn about politics, current events, law, and justice and to put their skills to the test.

Adolescents are notorious for demanding academic relevance. If learning isn't directly connected to their lives, why should they care? And how is school preparing them for being an adult?

Using the place-based model, we can extend the curricular relevance even further by working with community members to create authentic projects with real outcomes. Students are learning career skills and lending their talents and knowledge to local improvement efforts. This is a very different approach from traditional middle school, which does not usually offer avenues for adolescents to develop their interests and abilities outside of school.

Over and over again, we have seen kids who came to our school as disinterested learners transform into involved, engaged students. When we are doing real work, there are fewer questions as to why we are doing what we are doing. The kids aren't simply turning homework in for their teachers to grade; the audience lies beyond the classroom walls, in the "real world." It is incredibly empowering for adolescents to know that the adult community values their work.

There are many examples of middle school place-based projects throughout this book, and a couple more included here. This chapter mainly focuses on how to further prepare students for civic engagement and stewardship in 7th and 8th grade classrooms.

CONFLICT AS A CENTRAL THEME IN MIDDLE SCHOOL CIVIC EDUCATION

Conflict in middle school is unavoidable. Students challenge their parents, their teachers, and each other. They are ready to learn about war and other disagreements, but they need a lot of scaffolding to help them understand the nuances. Learning how to consider all sides of an issue is an enormously valuable skill to bring into their lives as democratic citizens. Knowing how to make a clear, persuasive argument is a skill they will need as they begin to advocate for their communities.

This means that teachers need to be prepared to tackle difficult topics. Students will often come into a class with strong, already established opinions. Or sometimes a topic will seem so cut-and-dry to them that they will immediately commit to a side before learning more. Teachers have the opportunity to give students the tools they need to slow down, consider different perspectives, gather evidence, and craft cohesive arguments. This is where civil discourse comes into play.

Immigration

Immigration can be a touchy topic. For middle school students tuning into recent news, there are lots of questions: Why is there so much debate about immigration? Where are immigrants coming from and why? How come some people don't want them here while others are defending them? The discussion can become tremendously personal depending on the student population. It is important for teachers to be aware of recent immigrants in their class, or students who have family members who are immigrants, and facilitate with care and compassion. Plus, someone with firsthand experience can be an invaluable resource!

Our 7th and 8th graders explored questions surrounding American immigration policy in a trimester-long study. As part of this study, students went on two walking tours of historical immigrant neighborhoods in Portland: Japantown and South Portland. A local immigration lawyer came in to the class to talk about her work and about current policy. Other guest speakers included the head of the Human Trafficking Task Force in Portland and a representative from Portland's Immigration and Refugee Community Organization.

In addition to learning about the history of national policy, students participated in a Storyline where they assumed the identities of different stakeholders within the debate. This allowed them to think more personally about all sides of the issue. The classes also read the nonfiction account *Enrique's Journey*, by Sonia Nazario, to learn the intimate details of one individual's odyssey from Honduras to the United States.

As a culminating event, students hosted a naturalization ceremony at school. The middle schoolers welcomed 10 new citizens to the United States by decorating the room, providing food and drink for a reception, and singing the national anthem. After the ceremony, students had the opportunity to interview the new residents and hear their stories. Two newspapers covered the event, and several of the parents who attended commented on how powerful the experience was for them and their children.

The First Amendment

One of the most common student misconceptions about the Bill of Rights is that the First Amendment gives them the right to say whatever they want. Students hide behind this fallacy as an excuse to use profanity or justification when they verbally offend their peers. What they don't always know is that every right comes with responsibilities. Although the freedom of speech is one of the fundamental facts we want our students to know, it is equally important for them to learn about the limitations of the First Amendment.

Recently, we taught about these restrictions by studying court cases where the First Amendment was called into question. Students broke up into small groups, studied specific cases, and then presented their findings to the class. One important case, *Chaplinsky v. New Hampshire*, was when the Supreme Court laid out the "fighting words" doctrine: words that are so offensive that they incite violence, or lead to a breach of the peace, should not be protected by the First Amendment.

We also talked about the meaning of *libel* and *slander* and tied these ideas to the life of a middle school student. The students learned that spreading rumors is akin to slander and that it is not legal to spread lies that can ruin someone's reputation. They learned that, as a nation, we have decided that severely hurtful or intimidating speech is not worthy of protection.

At the same time, the Supreme Court sometimes rules to protect speech that most people find horribly offensive. In the 2011 case *Snyder v. Phelps*, the court decided to protect the Westboro Baptist Church's picketing of military funerals. Even though the signs were incredibly hurtful and offensive, the court decided that the protests did not interfere with the funerals, and therefore were not disruptive. This opened up a conversation about the difference between what is legally permitted and what just seems socially or morally wrong.

Most students passionately disagreed with the Supreme Court on the Westboro Baptist Church ruling, leading to a conversation about hate speech in general. Should it be legal or illegal? Why? What about in our school? What words would we consider hateful? How can students be held accountable for what they say? Should we have a code against hate speech?

By the end of this unit, none of the students could say that the First Amendment gives them the right to say whatever they want. As citizens of a democracy, it is our shared responsibility to recognize how words can impinge upon the rights of others.

Elections

Another potentially volatile, but vital, topic to teach is political elections. Many students, like their parents, come into these conversations with their minds already made up; the point of the exchange isn't so much to gather new information as it is to sway the other person. This can make for uncomfortable situations in the classroom, just as it does for adults in the workplace or at social gatherings.

We encourage our students to try and learn as much about a candidate as possible instead of just aligning themselves with their parents' beliefs. As they reach adulthood, it is time for young people to start making their own decisions. We discuss what factors a citizen takes into consideration when deciding who to vote for: a candidate's platform, their party affiliation, their record, their personal background, and their campaign. We also spend a good deal of time investigating the character trait of leadership and considering what makes a good leader.

We make sure that our students pay attention to national, state, and local elections. In Portland and in Oregon, some of the most contentious matters are decided by ballot measure. Learning about these measures is a great way for students to become familiar with current events, local issues, and popular democracy. Investigating local government also creates opportunities for field trips to city hall, the state capitol, and the office in charge of elections.

The art of civil discourse comes into play when discussing politics in the classroom. It is essential that students use evidence to back up their arguments. This is a good opportunity for teachers to lead lessons on finding credible sources and why that practice is so important. See chapter 6 for more about civil discourse.

Other relevant but difficult topics include race, homelessness, gender identity, sexism, and more. Many of these issues are embedded in local and national conflicts. As teachers, we need to help our students begin to unpack the complexity and understand all of the different factors leading to disagreement.

These issues are not exclusive to the realm of social studies. We have also addressed local conflict in our science program. Studying problems between humans and animals is a great way to explore ecology because it is often a hook for students. In Oregon, sea lions have been pitted against fishermen, wolves against ranchers, and coyotes against pet owners. We have investigated all of these disputes by reading newspaper articles and scientific research, inviting experts into the classroom, writing letters to editors, simulating town meetings, and holding debates.

INCREASED INTERACTION WITH THE COMMUNITY
THROUGH INTERNSHIPS

Engaging with the wider community is a key element in building a strong place-based middle school program. This is where students can put their career skills in practice and develop a work ethic. Now that they are older, their talents and abilities have increased value and students can meet local needs on a more complex level.

Every spring, our 8th graders fan out across the school, the neighborhood, and the city to volunteer in classrooms, nonprofit organizations, and businesses. In the past, students have interned at retirement centers, computer recycling centers, soup kitchens, the Red Cross, local watershed councils, classrooms, and many more locations.

Internships take place one afternoon a week during the spring trimester. Parents and students receive information about their placement along with permission slips and a behavior contract approximately two weeks before the program begins. In addition to hands-on service work, students also reflect on their experience through guided journal questions and class discussion.

Because students go to their internship site over the course of the eight weeks, they have the opportunity to build a relationship with that particular community partner while also learning more about the service that partner provides. When we are able, we also place students in internships that highlight their special interests or skills.

For the last couple of years, the retirement home a few blocks from the school has requested students who can serve as technology teachers. The students are stationed in the computer room and residents come to them with questions about their smartphones, tablets, and laptops. The seniors have given us incredibly positive feedback about this internship, and the students have a chance to share and show off their tech skills. Without knowing it, they are gaining experience in communication and problem-solving.

SERVICE IN THE SCHOOL

Service isn't interacting only with adults; it also means creating healthy connections with younger children. In the traditional middle school model, adolescents and elementary-age kids have no contact with one another. Perhaps the older students feel more "adult" because they are with kids their own age, but there is less of a tangible reason for them to *act* like adults. The opportunity for students to relate to younger children gives them a chance to engage with a different dynamic, one that can empower them while also bringing a stronger sense of community to the school (photo 9.1).

A K–8 school offers countless opportunities for adolescents to take leadership roles. They can function as tutors, reading buddies, teachers, and role models. Students throughout our school build stronger relationships, and middle school students have a chance to move beyond their peer group.

Students who do not always have the best interactions with people their own age can thrive in a leadership role in a younger class. We have seen depressed students glow with pride when they return from the kindergarten classroom, hands full of cards declaring, "I love you!" For some students, this is the first time they have ever succeeded in a

Photo 9.1.   *A 7th grader guides a kindergartener through Portland's Oaks Bottom Wildlife Refuge.*
Photo by Emily Conner

leadership role. It can change the way they think about themselves and increase their confidence. Such growth would not be possible if they were not permitted to interact with younger kids.

Project Citizen

At the Cottonwood School, we have adopted a program for our 7th and 8th grade students designed by the Center for Civic Education called Project Citizen (PC). This has been a perfect place-based unit for middle school, as it integrates civic education, civic action, and service, along with multiple standard-based skills. The idea is simple: identify a local problem, research it, propose a policy-based solution, and put the solution into action. Simply put, Project Citizen is a formula for citizen participation in creating public policy.

Admittedly, public policy is not the most exciting topic for middle school students, especially when taught traditionally. But Project Citizen invites kids into a realm that they assume is reserved for select adults and, by doing so, encourages them to be active contributors to the decision-making process in their community. Project Citizen is often the unit our students like the best, probably because it is the unit that empowers them the most.

The first step in all PC units is identifying community problems. Students do this in different ways: reading newspaper articles, revisiting topics they've studied in class, or interviewing people. Our students interview two people each—one has to be an adult and one can be under 18. They ask them what they think is the biggest problem in their community. Some years we limit the definition of *community* to mean the small neighborhood where our school is located or even just the school. Some years, we open it up to mean the entire city.

Next, we share all the problems we collected and look for overlaps. This usually gives us a pool of up to 50 issues.

Students then divide into small groups and put each issue through a four-question filter to see if it would be a "good" problem for PC. The questions are:

1. Does government have a responsibility to deal with it?
2. Is the problem important to our community and our class?

Photo 9.2. Surveying neighborhood residents for Project Citizen.
Photo by author

3. Is there enough information to gather about the problem?
4. Is it a problem that we might be able to solve?

After reporting back and allowing for some group discussion, we narrow our list down to six or seven problems.

Students sign up to research one of the chosen issues. For the next several days, they look for information online, call local agencies, and conduct interviews and surveys in the neighborhood and school (photo 9.2). At the end of the week, each group presents a poster outlining their issue and explains why it is the problem the class should choose. After all groups have presented, the class votes.

Once students have selected the problem, they check to see if there are any unanswered questions to research. Then they brainstorm solutions. This is a similar process to when they chose a problem, but not as lengthy. Small groups research and present what they found. This time, the class needs to come to a consensus, which means there is more discussion, persuasion, and negotiation before they reach a final solution.

The last step is creating an action plan. Students identify what they need to do in order to make their solution a reality and who they need to recruit as supporters.

One of the culminating events for PC in Oregon is when students present their project at a showcase at the state capitol organized by the local nonprofit organization Classroom Law Project. In order to prepare for the presentation, students focus on different aspects of what's called the "portfolio." Some students create artwork to illustrate the problem on a four-panel display board, while others write reports to communicate their research and proposals and another group designs graphs and charts to show off the survey results. Another group of students creates a binder full of all of our research and notes from our meetings, while still another small group launches our solution into action. This stage takes full advantage of the range of students' talents and interests; kids who are passionate about art, math, writing, or organization all have a way to contribute their strength.

On the day of the showcase, a group of representatives gives an oral presentation to a panel of judges at the state house, which is also when the first place winner is revealed (photo 9.3). But this is not usually the end of the project. Because this is a real-world problem that we are addressing, the class works on it up until the end of the school year.

Photo 9.3.   *7th-grade students present their Project Citizen portfolio at the Oregon capitol.*
Photo by Peter DeLap

Over the past few years, our students have researched myriad initial problems that passed the first four-question test, such as river pollution, bike safety, lack of e-cigarette regulation, empty lots in the neighborhood, and the need for a school cafeteria. Some of the finalists we brought to the state showcase include dog owners not picking up after their pets, too many miles of unpaved city streets, need for a later school start time, and need for a better playground at our school.

One year, the 7th-grade class voted to explore smoking in public parks. It turned out to be the right issue at the right time because the city council had recently decided to look into the matter. Students surveyed people in the neighborhood, found online research about secondhand smoke, contacted health advocacy agencies such as the American Lung Association and the American Heart Association, and started a petition.

One student found an article about a state representative who had proposed a bill to the Oregon legislature to ban cigarettes statewide. Needless to say, the bill did not pass, but we thought the congressman might support the class effort. Indeed, the representative visited our class to speak of his experience and answer questions. He even wrote a letter of support, as did the health advocacy organizations we contacted. The students' cause was highlighted in the city newspaper and their online petition garnered hundreds of signatures.

The project's display and presentation won them a first place ribbon in the PC competition at the state capitol. As exhilarating as that was, the victory wasn't the highlight. We were invited to Portland City Hall by the city commissioner in charge of parks to give our presentation. Again, the city paper covered the story, and the commissioner asked us to return the following year when the bill would be up for vote to give testimony to the entire council. The students' pride was palpable.

Through the PC process, students learned what it means to be a member of a democratic society where citizens take an active part in governing. This is exactly what we should be teaching kids in public education. In order to maintain a democratic system, it is essential that our young people know how to access government. Part of this means demystifying public policy and showing them that they are indeed powerful and capable. It is not just the rich or adults who can make change in our cities and communities; it can even be a group of passionate 13-year-olds.

EXTENDING EXPLORATIONS

Middle school students are eager and ready to explore the world beyond city limits. In our 7th-and 8th-grade program, we include overnight trips as part of the curriculum. The trips generally take place toward the end of the year, but we also go on community-building retreats in September (photo 9.4).

The location of our end-of-year trip alternates on a two-year cycle: one has an urban focus and the other brings students to the wilderness. There are several reasons why we incorporate overnight trips into our curriculum:

1. To build deeper community between students and teachers, and across grades
2. To foster a stronger understanding of environment, whether urban or wild
3. To nurture a stronger connection to place

Photo 9.4.   Middle school students have more opportunities to explore the world outside of the city limits. Here, an 8th grader navigates a tide pool on the Oregon coast.
Photo by author

4. To reinforce and build on the curriculum taught in class
5. To encourage personal growth and reflection through new experiences
6. To disrupt normal routines and create possibilities for positive change

Overnight trips are part of our curriculum; they are not an add-on. Student attendance is required. They do cost money, which we ask parents to pay, but we also offer payment plans and scholarships, and parents can organize fundraisers. We have never left a child behind because they could not pay.

In the urban-centered years, students go to Seattle, our sister city. Students take the Amtrak north and stay in a youth hostel located in the International District. From there, they visit Pike Place Market, the aquarium, and the Seattle Center; take a tour of historic Chinatown and Japantown; take a ferry to Bainbridge Island; and visit the Klondike Gold Rush museum.

This trip gives students the opportunity to compare and contrast Seattle's history and culture with Portland's. This may be the first time they have stayed in a downtown area or taken the Amtrak without their parents, and for most, it's the first time they have stayed in an international hostel and been surrounded by people of different nationalities.

For our wilderness rotation, we have been very happy to partner with Outward Bound. On this trip, students travel to the high desert in Central Oregon and camp out near a unique geological feature called Smith Rock. Here, students learn the basics of rock climbing and rappelling. This kind of physical challenge can build self-confidence by pushing students beyond their comfort zones in a safe and supportive way.

Placed-based education serves middle school students well. It facilitates their integration into adulthood and validates their questions and concerns about the world around them. When we allow our adolescent students to engage in the difficult topics of real life, we communicate to them that we respect their opinions and trust their ability to comprehend and respond to complex material. We further empower them as young citizens by channeling their desire to be a part of the adult world into meaningful service work and opportunities to travel beyond the familiar.

As with the primary grades, intentionally aligning the program with the students' developmental needs is how we make place-based education most successful.

RESOURCES

The main website for Project Citizen is http://www.civiced.org/pro grams/project-citizen. Here you can find links to the programs in your state.

The World We Want, directed by Patrick Davidson (2010), provides a wonderfully inspirational overview of the Project Citizen process. The director follows students around the world as they create projects and ultimately come together in Washington, DC, for an international showcase. The DVD comes with a 25-minute condensed version that is perfect to show a class at the beginning of the project.

The Kid's Guide to Social Action: How to Solve the Social Problems You Choose—and Turn Creative Thinking into Positive Action by Barbara A. Lewis (1998) is a great resource in any classroom, but is especially helpful in the middle school classroom. Lewis gives kids step-by-step instructions on how to launch civic action projects with tools such as writing petitions, crafting letters to the editor, and proposing changes to laws.

The Project Citizen section of this chapter is adapted from a version previously published by *Community Works Journal*. http://www.communityworksinstitute.org/cwjonline/articles/aarticles -text/anderson_civics.html

CHAPTER 10

Implementing Place-Based Education: Crucial Questions

Some educators may argue that place-based learning sounds great in theory, but there are too many challenges for it to be a realistic school model. It is true that limited funding, standardized testing, and overextended schedules are all real hurdles to implementation. But the benefits of this teaching approach outweigh the difficulties, and the more a teacher practices, the easier it becomes. Teachers eager to develop projects or try place-based education in their schools have many of the same questions. This chapter attempts to answer some of them.

"I want to create a place-based project in my classroom, but I'm not sure where to start."

Because few schools in the United States have place-based education embedded in their mission, many teachers who attempt these sorts of projects in their classrooms are acting either alone or perhaps in collaboration with a small cohort. If this is the case, they probably do not have structural support like a fieldwork coordinator or even an administrator who will go out of their way to make things happen. Without a Community to Vision Forum to identify goals or a support person to create partnerships, much of the legwork falls on the classroom teacher.

The best advice is to start small. What area in your curriculum can you connect to place? When you think of "place," think history, people, businesses, careers, land areas, bodies of water, natural resource issues, and your own students. Can you better illustrate what you are teaching by giving students local examples or hands-on experience in their community?

Taking a field trip, inviting in guest speakers, and investigating articles from local newspapers are all great first steps, and maybe that's as far as you will get the first year.

If and when you have more energy and resources to add additional elements, the next question to tackle is "Who can we help?" Remember, service learning is an essential component of place-based education, so at some point you'll need to find a way to get your students working with and helping the community. What organizations, agencies, groups, or businesses might have a vested interest in the topic you are studying? Might their goals somehow align with yours as an educator? Are they already working with youth groups in some way?

Identify potential partners and reach out. Attend meetings of organizations that are dealing with social or environmental issues in your community. Go to neighborhood association meetings and meetings of the county sustainability committee if there is one. You may discover the perfect project. This is part of how you transform your role from classroom teacher to engaged citizen and community liaison.

Summer is a key time for teachers to develop place-based projects for the following year. It is when teachers have more time to devote to long-term planning. It may also be when some teachers can put aside time to research at the local historical society, take a class on native plants, or delve into the workings of city government. Setting up a project with a partner can take months; it is always a good idea to allow as much time as possible for these projects to come together. Once the school year begins, it is often difficult to find the needed time to lay a strong foundation. Starting small the year before can make it easier to develop and strengthen a curricular unit in phases instead of creating it all at one time from scratch.

"What are the essential components of a place-based school?"

Most schools that are truly practicing place-based learning will incorporate the following five elements:

1. **Service learning.** A key component of place-based education is making community service a regular part of the learning process. When we develop projects, we ask the question "What

does our community need?" in addition to outlining what our students need to know. Student work is not just for the teacher, but a way for the student to more fully engage with community members and organizations while learning deeply about a topic or issue. Additionally, the service is not just an add-on, but is integrated into the overall project curriculum: this is the "learning" part of service learning.

2. **Long-term community partners.** Long-term relationships help us to become more involved and invested in our community and allow us to fulfill our mission of providing authentic work for students. These relationships can take several years to develop, but they are critical for creating a stable program. Working with partner agencies and organizations also ensures civic engagement and authentic audiences.

3. **Fieldwork.** Fieldwork is not the same as going on field trips. Field trips enhance learning in the classroom; fieldwork is learning in action: the data collection, observation, and interviewing that students need to gain information about a topic and complete a project. When students go into the field to work, they are using their community as a laboratory; the world outside the school *becomes* the classroom.

4. **Knowing our environment.** One of the intended outcomes of place-based education is for students to have a better understanding and appreciation of their natural environment. Earth and life sciences are front and center in the science curriculum.

5. **Knowing our history.** Another one of the intended outcomes of place-based education is for students to have a better understanding and appreciation of their local history. This means that we focus on local topics, but we also try to find and highlight the natural connections between national/global history and our local story.

"How do I know if my project is place-based, if it is project-based, experiential, or one of the other educational approaches mentioned at the beginning of this book?"

As mentioned earlier, place-based education incorporates and overlaps with several other methods and strategies. A teacher could lead a unit on their local community that is still not a place-based project. Below is an outline of the layers involved in a place-based unit, starting from the shared goal of teaching about place. Each layer includes and builds on the previous layer. You could even think of this as a checklist of the elements of a place-based project.

Layer 1: Learning about place is a curricular goal
Layer 2: Content- or skills-based unit
- Incorporates some experiential learning
- Combines several lessons and activities around one topic
- Includes a culminating project

Layer 3: An integrated learning unit focused on content or skills
- Combines several lessons and activities around one topic
- Includes a culminating project
- Integrates two or more subjects: writing, reading, social studies, science, art, etc.

Layer 4: Project-based unit
- Includes more youth voice and fieldwork, and extends to audiences outside of the classroom
- The project is framed by a meaningful problem to solve or a question to answer
- The project features real-world context, tasks and tools, quality standards, or impact—or speaks to students' personal concerns, interests, and issues in their lives
- Students make some decisions about the project, including how they work and what they create
- Students make their project work public by explaining, displaying, and/or presenting it to people beyond the classroom

Layer 5: Place-based project
- Community partner and service learning are key
- Incorporates extensive fieldwork
- Addresses the question: How are you increasing the livability of the community?

"What is my role as a teacher in a place-based classroom?"

At the Cottonwood School, it takes many of our teachers two or three years before they feel comfortable designing and leading place-based projects. Many teachers are trained to work in traditional classrooms in conventionally structured schools. It can be difficult to shift their understanding of the teacher's role in a place-based classroom, and sometimes it can be scary. Pat Willis and Susan Cross explain how the role of a teacher may change:

> You may find yourself much more of a coordinator and learning manager than a deliverer of set curriculum. You may find that the most important function you can serve is finding access for your students to partnership opportunities with other adult instructors. You may spend your time locating project ideas, equipment and funds rather than directly teaching lessons. You may need to spend time on the phone coordinating an event or writing proposals to fund your program's newsletter. It is not the role you are probably most familiar with and it can seem like a leap into the unknown. It can also lead to personal growth and a great deal of fulfillment as your program blossoms.[1]

Another way to think of yourself in the classroom is as a "connecter." You are connecting students to the community and to each other, and helping them associate curricular content to their lives and where they live.

Of course, there will still be many traditional aspects to your position: creating assessments, providing structure and discipline, planning lessons, and adhering to standards. But place-based learning will probably happen more organically if you see your role as a facilitator instead of being someone who gives information and needs to know all of the answers.

"How do I prepare my classroom for place-based projects? What materials will I need?"

When setting up your classroom, think about what you will need for a variety of purposes such as small group work, interviewing a guest speaker, or building space for a large 3-D map. Here are a few materials that can be especially helpful in a place-based classroom:

- Clipboards: Having lots of clipboards on hand is essential for small group work, conducting surveys in the neighborhood, and collecting data in the field. Find a way to keep track of them; they are used so often that they tend to disappear!

- A phone with a speaker option: Almost all classrooms have phones, so this should be an easy one. Phones are needed to call partners or to find out information from local agencies. We also use them for conference calls with guest speakers when they can't make it into the classroom.
- Furniture that is easy to rearrange or cluster: This can help you move quickly between small student work groups and a whole-class meeting. Having tables that collapse also allows more room for you to create a circle of chairs or rows of chairs for an audience.
- A digital camera: Photos can help tell your story and are necessary to create products for some projects.
- A digital audio recorder: It is great to have a recorder on hand (and a few students trained on how to use it) to capture interviews, guest speakers, and project notes. Some smartphone apps might serve your purpose.

"What is the best way to assess student work in a place-based school system?"

Place-based unit work can be assessed just like any other student learning. This means applying best practices to receive the most valuable feedback on how your students are learning. The teacher's guide *Connecting Service Learning to the Curriculum* articulates that, "Practiced at its best, assessment invites students into the learning process: How are we doing? Where can we go from here? We can easily explain progress or lack of it to students and parents when we can point to standards we and the students agreed to target, and show concrete examples of what achievement looks like."[2]

What you assess depends on your specific learning goals for a particular unit. In order to maintain clarity about what is expected from students, create different forms of assessment for different learning goals. This helps you collect evidence from more than one source, allowing you to get a more accurate picture of how a student has progressed. For example, during the watershed project where students were creating models to replace an outdated culvert, we could:

- Ask students to create a labeled diagram (including vocabulary words) to check their understanding of the water cycle

- Collect a series of checklists and feedback forms to see how they were doing with collaboration and communication within their small group
- Complete a rubric that captured their understanding of basic engineering and design
- Write comments (perhaps also with a rubric or scoring tool) in response to letters to the editor that students crafted about the culvert problem (persuasive writing).

Do not wait until the end of the unit to assess students. Instead, sprinkle assessment throughout the project in order to give kids and teachers immediate feedback on how things are going.

Other tips to keep in mind:

- Teachers and students can create criteria together for what a successful end result should look like—often in the form of a rubric.
- Give kids a choice in how they demonstrate progress, making sure to distinguish between their ability to communicate their learning and the learning itself.
- Include products and performances that allow for multiple intelligences and learning styles.

"What happens when difficult topics arise?"

When you open up your classroom and curriculum to the wider community, you are also inviting students to discover and grapple with difficult topics. Current events are full of complex issues, some of them rooted in a long history of inequity, conflict, or even violence. When we study the history of African Americans in Portland, we inevitably encounter and lead discussions about racism, police brutality, and redlining. When we teach our 1st and 2nd graders about food sources, students want to know why some people can afford food while other can't.

Some topics, like the ones mentioned above, give us valuable opportunities to address issues related to social justice. Other times, students stumble onto subjects that initially seem too "adult." For example, one of our 7th grade classes designed a Project Citizen project around the topic of strip clubs in their neighborhood. Other place-based classrooms have explored the wine industry, which is booming in Oregon, even though it made some parents uncomfortable that their children were learning about alcohol.

Difficult topics are a part of real life. Instead of shying away from them, it is important that we model for our students how to engage the content with maturity and curiosity. When students see that you are not reacting negatively, they will appreciate that you respect and trust them. The degree to which you delve into the topic depends both on the scope of your project and the age of your students. But generally, the more you are willing to unpack and uncover, the less taboo the subject becomes and the more informed your students will be.

When an uncomfortable or difficult topic arises, look for where the learning could take place. Is it an essential aspect of your overall topic? Is it an important issue in your local community? Do your students have a lot of authentic interest in the topic? If yes, then it may be worth it to spend more time with it. Not all of the learning needs to come from you. Think about local organizations working with this topic that could send a representative into the classroom or host a field trip. Or look for organizations that provide educators with curriculum to support class-room activities and discussions.

Teaching our students how to address topics that are traditionally re-served for the adult world will only help them become critical thinkers as well as active, engaged members of their communities.

"My school doesn't have funding for field trips.
How can I do fieldwork?"

As schools struggle with reduced funding, face increased pressure to "teach to the test," and find themselves with larger class sizes, field trips have slid down the priority list. Even at a school as small as the Cottonwood School, fieldwork can be difficult to coordinate since we do not have a school bus and bus rentals are expensive.

But this doesn't mean that you can't do fieldwork. The easiest way to get around the transportation issue is to select a study area within walk-ing distance. This may mean the local neighborhood, the nearby forest, or even school grounds. You may still need to recruit some chaperones to help "herd" the students, but you will not need to rent a bus.

If you are in an urban area—or even suburban, in some cases—you can look into taking public transit. Learning how to take public buses and trains is a valuable life skill for all children, and many cities provide discounts for school groups.

If you don't have public transit and you can't walk to your destination, there are some small grants out there specifically for field trips. Summer is a good time to investigate these possibilities, and the applications are usually simple. Some teachers have even taken the matter into their own hands and run GoFundMe campaigns to support fieldwork in their classrooms.

If fieldwork just isn't a possibility because of schedule or other logistics, the next best thing is to bring the community to your classroom. Welcome in guest experts, speaker panels, and people willing to be interviewed or surveyed. For those classrooms that can support technological options, you can host video conferences with experts or at least conference calls on a phone.

"I teach 200 students over five different class periods. Is there any way I can bring place-based education into my curriculum?"

The short but indeterminate answer is maybe. It will certainly be more difficult than if you are working with only one or two groups of students. Connecting to authentic service learning over an extended period of time will be the trickiest part.

Because the coordination piece will be complicated and time-consuming, it may be a good idea to begin small. Perhaps the first year starts with just one class and then builds on your successes. This is also a good way to grow a relationship with a partner. Once they know you better and have seen that you are trustworthy and capable, they may be more willing to devote additional time and resources to your project and relationship. Another option would be to create an elective class that includes place-based components—this is often possible for more experienced teachers.

There are certainly large groups of students that have taken on place-based projects, whether it be an entire K–6 school or all sections of 8th grade science. The Cottonwood School's "Adopt-a-Place" program is a good example of a whole-school partnership between us and Portland Parks and Recreation.

If you feel up to the challenge, you will require active support from your administration and some (or all!) of your co-teachers. You will also need a very structured partnership plan in place. It may take an entire school year—or even longer—just to design the project, attain the resources, and secure participants. There is plenty of work to do before students even get involved. Planning should also include the drafting of partnership agreements so that both partners are clear on their goals and responsibilities.

"I am under a lot of pressure to teach to the standards. Can I still incorporate place-based education?"

Absolutely! Nothing prevents place-based projects from being standards-based. Especially now that standards (especially NGSS) are trending toward skills, place-based projects can be an optimal way for students to learn standard-based skills as well as content.

In the book *Place-Based Curriculum Design: Exceeding Standards through Local Investigations*, author Amy B. Demarest suggests that locally based projects are not in conflict with a curriculum that is drawn from state and national standards. She contends that a place-based approach could even heighten student success on tests: "A larger purpose can house the mastery of the skills and knowledge of specific subjects—as well as bigger, more important questions. . . . Authentic investigations can foster higher-order thinking, authentic problem-solving and a cognitive richness that promotes academic achievement."[3]

Demarest states that place-based work and standards are most closely aligned when "assessment goals are clearly defined."[4] As stated above, there is little difference between evaluating skills and content within a place-based unit and assessment within a traditional unit. When done well, it is focused and clearly tied to the standards.

Place-based curriculum design can feel foreign and sometimes uncomfortable to teachers whose primary experience is in the traditional classroom. If this is the case, start with a mini-project and work with a few targeted standards. Once you start a project, you may also find connections to other unexpected cross-curricular standards (like the engineering project that came out of a watershed study).

If you teach one content area, consider collaborating with other teachers to create an interdisciplinary project. Although this can be logistically tricky, it is a good way to maximize your time while optimizing your project for standards connection.

State or national standards may even be the starting point for creating a place-based program. As Demarest points out, "Standards can provide the basis for whole-school and district-wide reorientation to the local environment."[5]

"Can place-based education be considered rigorous?"

The word *rigor* is thrown around often these days by administrators, teachers, and parents alike. But what does it mean?

There doesn't seem to be a clearly agreed-upon definition of "rigorous" schoolwork,[6] although in a loose sense, it seems to mean "high level" (middle schoolers learning high school material), challenging, and (sometimes) just more difficult. This corresponds with a more traditional conception of academics in a direct instruction classroom.

However, if we hone our understanding of *rigor*, it can easily be applied to place-based curriculum and classrooms. In place-based classrooms, students are challenged and engaged while also being intellectually and socially stimulated. You will not see students taking pages of notes from a lecture, completing hours of homework a night, or buckling down with a textbook, but these do not need to be indicators of rigor.

Students in a place-based classroom are pushed and challenged in ways other students are not. When we ask students to solve problems, think critically, work collaboratively, communicate effectively with adult community partners, and manage timelines, we teach them valuable skills while providing engaging projects and opportunities for them to build and develop the skills that are most meaningful to them. Such an education can certainly be considered rigorous.

"How does placed-based education address the need for equity in our schools? How can it help close the achievement gap?"

Place-based projects provide many ways for students to see their own experience reflected in what they are learning. Because students are studying their neighborhoods, towns, and cities, they are able to incorporate their own experience into the curriculum. When teachers ask students to identify problems in their communities and work toward finding solutions, young people are given an opportunity to bring their prior knowledge and background into the classroom. As teachers and students explore issues around inequity in their communities, they will find many opportunities to integrate social justice into the curriculum.

When teachers take the time to build community, get to know their students, and allow the students to really get to know each other, all practices important in place-based classrooms, they are able to set the groundwork for an environment that is truly culturally responsive. Building an atmosphere of trust and respect is key when asking students to share experiences from their life outside of school. And since closing the achievement gap means eliminating schools that feel "culturally unfriendly,"[7] this is imperative work.

One commonly suggested cause of the achievement gap is school's lack of relevancy for many students.[8] Through research conducted by the Place-Based Education Evaluation Collaborative, students reported being more engaged in place-based projects versus traditional classroom projects.[9] Helping students to see a direct connection between their lives, their school, and their future can keep students interested while simultaneously creating a more inclusive environment.

"I am already overextended as a teacher. How can I possibly add more?"

Again, the advice here is "start small, go slow." You don't need to recreate the wheel or overhaul your entire curriculum in one year. Begin with a small project, or with local connections to familiar curriculum. Allow yourself time for development.

Another important thing to keep in mind is that place-based education is not intended to be an add-on. When implemented properly, the place-based approach is integrated into the existing curriculum, not shoehorned into an additional time slot. By linking your primary subjects to the place-based projects, you are simply shifting the focus from individual skills to an interconnected unit.

This isn't to say that there won't be extra tasks involved with leading a place-based unit, such as coordinating fieldwork, reaching out to guest speakers, and building a partnership. The best advice here is, if possible, recruit help! Are there parents who would like to be more involved? Or a student teacher or intern? Sometime students in the older grades can even help make phone calls and set up speakers. Think of it as a collaborative experiment and do what you can to try and have fun!

Our world has undergone immense change since the proliferation of public school in the mid-19th century. Many of our local economies are reeling from the effects of globalization. Personal technology captures our attention and allows us to ignore what is right in front of us. A climate of fear keeps our kids from exploring the natural world independently and even prevents us from getting to know our neighbors. Social and environmental injustice continue to be widespread. The coming years feel uncertain.

We are in dire need of educational models that work to create a hopeful future. Children must reconnect with the people and the land in the places where they live. Adults can model collaboration and compassion, empowering students to build the world they want. Schools, the epicenters of many communities, can begin a ripple effect for positive change.

Embracing place-based education requires teachers to become advocates. Administrators, colleagues, and even parents may resist any approach that feels unfamiliar or challenges traditional ways of doing things. Interested teachers can prepare for this pushback by collecting materials that testify to the advantages of the model. The Place-Based Education Evaluation Collaborative has done excellent work gathering research targeting common concerns around academic achievement. Once a school experiences a successful project, the benefits speak for themselves.

There has been good news recently for place-based education. Revised standards increasingly support experiential learning and real-world skills. Authentic, project-based learning has even been referred to as the way of the future.[10] Graduate teaching programs reference the model, and place-based education is getting more exposure in blogs and nonprofit newsletters (see a couple of examples in the Resources section at the end of this chapter).

As place-based education gains more attention, however, it is important that we proceed with caution. By nature, the approach is not something that can be mass-produced or simplified to a series of classroom lessons or activities. It is not a small alteration to "education as usual," nor is it an add-on. We need to protect the heart of place-based education through this transition. One innovative teacher at a time, and one school at a time, we can impart to our children the skills and experience required to build not only the future we want, but the future we need.

RESOURCES

The Place-Based Evaluation Collaborative has collected several studies speaking to the benefits of place-based education: http://www.peec-works.org/index. Included on the website is a brochure that highlights some of the primary points:
http://www.peecworks.org/PEEC/Benefits_of_PBE-PEEC_2008_webpdf.

The learning design firm Getting Smart created a blog to document place-based projects.
http://www.gettingsmart.com/categories/series/place-based-education/

The March 2017 online newsletter from the Green Schools National Network was dedicated to examples of place-based education from around the country.
https://greenschoolsnationalnetwork.org/news/

The Teton Science Schools have been collecting research about their place-based programing.
https://www.tetonscience.org/index.cfm?id=innovation-educational-research

NOTES

1. Willis, Patrick, and Susan Cross. 2014. "Starting a Community-Based Natural Resource Education Program." *Clearing*, June 13. Accessed February 18, 2017. http://clearingmagazine.org/archives/10042.

2. Brooks, Joe, Susan Bonthron, and Mary Azarian. 2005. *Connecting Service Learning to the Curriculum: A Workbook for Teachers and Administrators.* Los Angeles: Community Works Institute Press, 37.

3. Demarest, Amy B. 2015. *Place-Based Curriculum Design: Exceeding Standards through Local Investigations.* New York: Routledge, 16–17.

4. Ibid., 16.

5. Ibid.

6. Sztabnik, Brian. 2015. "A New Definition of Rigor." *Edutopia*, May 7. Accessed February 18, 2017. https://www.edutopia.org/blog/a-new-defini tion-of-rigor-brian-sztabnik.

7. National Education Association. 2017. *Identifying Factors That Contribute to Achievement Gaps.* Accessed February 18, 2017. http://www.nea .org/home/17413.htm.

8. Bridgeland, John M., John J. Dilulio, and Karen Burke Morison. 2006. *The Silent Epidemic: Perspectives of High School Dropouts.* A report by Civic Enterprises in association with Peter D. Hart Research Associates for the Bill & Melinda Gates Foundation. Accessed February 18, 2017. http://www.ig nitelearning.com/pdf/TheSilentEpidemic3-06FINAL.pdf. McNulty, Raymond J., and Russell J. Quaglia. 2007. "Rigor, Relevance and Relationships: Three Passwords That Unlock the Door for Engaged High School Students to Learn at Appropriate Levels." *School Administrator* 64 (8). Accessed February 18, 2017. http://www.aasa.org/SchoolAdministratorArticle.aspx?id=6534. National Education Association, *Identifying Factors*.

9. Place-Based Education Evaluation Collaborative. 2010. *The Benefits of Place-Based Education: A Report from the Place-Based Education Evaluation Collaborative* (2nd ed.). Retrieved May 27, 2017. http://tinyurl.com/ PEECBrochure.

10. Eger, John M. 2016. "The Future of Learning: Project-Based, Place-Based, Experiential, Authentic, Constructivism." *HuffPost*, September 11. Accessed February 18, 2017. http://www.huffingtonpost.com/john-m-eger/the -future-of-learning-pr_b_11959832.html.

About the Author

Sarah K. Anderson holds a degree in American Studies from Bard College, and a MEd from Antioch New England Graduate School. Anderson taught 7th and 8th grade humanities at Key School in Annapolis, Maryland, and then at the Cottonwood School of Civics and Science in Portland, Oregon. Before teaching in the classroom, Anderson spent many years as an educator in nontraditional settings: she served as a community outreach coordinator for Metro Parks and Greenspaces in Portland, she taught job skills to local high school students on a farm in Vermont, and she worked as a teacher-naturalist in the California Redwoods. She is currently the fieldwork and place-based education coordinator at the Cottonwood School.

As part of the Cottonwood School's mission to disseminate place-based education practices to other schools in the Pacific Northwest, Anderson leads workshops and mentors other teachers in place-based curriculum design. She has also trained teachers around Oregon in Project Citizen, a program from the Center for Civic Education.

Anderson has written for *Teaching Tolerance*, *Educational Leadership*, and *Community Works Journal*, and her work has been featured by *Yes! Magazine*. She lives in Portland, Oregon, with her husband and young son.

Made in the USA
Las Vegas, NV
11 January 2022

41090743R00121